Divorce Is
a Family Affair

Divorce Is
a Family Affair

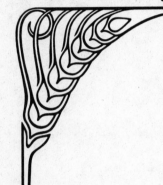

Margaret Johnson

ZONDERVAN
PUBLISHING HOUSE OF THE ZONDERVAN CORPORATION
GRAND RAPIDS, MICHIGAN 49506

DIVORCE IS A FAMILY AFFAIR
Copyright © 1983 by The Zondervan Corporation
Grand Rapids, Michigan

Some names have been changed to protect the privacy of the individuals
involved.

Library of Congress Cataloging in Publication Data

Johnson, Margaret.
  Divorce is a family affair.

    1. Divorce—United States—Religious aspects—
Christianity—Case studies.   2.   Family—United States—
Religious life—Case studies.   I.   Title.
HQ834.J43   1983   306.8'9   83-1109
ISBN 0-310-45831-5

Edited by Julie Ackerman Link
Designed by Donna Greenlee

Printed in the United States of America

83 84 85 86 87 88 89 90 — 10 9 8 7 6 5 4 3 2 1

To Dave,
for his understanding heart

Contents

Unless a kernel of wheat falls to the ground and dies, it remains only a single seed. But if it dies, it produces many seeds.

John 12:24

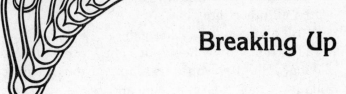

Chapter 1

Breaking Up

For a long time after the day of the phone call, I would associate it with heat, the sort of blistery heat that parches surrounding valleys without mercy, turning the mountainsides a deep red-brown, withering flowers before their time. In future years, heat and smog would automatically push the button of my memory.

When I answered the phone, Nancy, our oldest child, caught me off guard with shocking news. "Mom, I can't believe this is happening, but Doug has left me."

I froze in silence while she went on to tell me the details—why her husband of over ten years had left. Her sentences were quietly even but fragmented, as though she were talking to herself.

"He kept saying he had to leave, to find himself, time to get away and think." She paused. "He's been restless the past few weeks, but I never thought . . ."

In the background I could hear her two sons, four and seven, happily playing, unaware that their

9

world had been turned upside down. The sudden realization of what this would mean to them intercepted all other thoughts.

"Josh and Kev? . . ." I began.

"They don't know he's gone. They were outdoors playing." She went on to explain. "I took them to Sunday school this morning, and when we came home I knew . . . I knew something was wrong. Doug was restlessly pacing the floor. He wouldn't look at me, so I fed the boys and went into the den to study for my algebra exam. Then I noticed him leaning against the door. When I saw his face, I knew he was going to say something I didn't want to hear. Mom, there's another girl. Someone he met at work. They've been having dinner together the nights he didn't come home. He said . . . he said he loves her."

"Oh, Nancy." I clutched the telephone, suddenly chilled, forcing myself to listen in silence, though I was sure this must be a bad dream. I'll wake up any minute, I thought. But Nancy was still talking softly.

"He told me everything, mom. Sometimes he held me and cried, saying he was so sorry he had to hurt me, that he never meant this to happen. Then he went into the bedroom and threw his jeans and shirts into his duffel bag. And when he reached into the back of the closet for his *winter* jacket, I knew it was over. He's really gone."

"Nancy, you don't know that. Perhaps this is a passing affair that will be over soon. Maybe he simply needs time—time to get away and get himself together."

She didn't hear me. Her need to relive the afternoon's events forced her to continue.

"When he left he was wearing the blue shirt I had just bought for his birthday. I was so numb, I watched in a daze as he walked out the door. I dimly heard the boys calling after him, and then the truck started up and . . ."

When her voice broke, tears filled my eyes. I reached for a chair, wishing that its physical stability could bring me some emotional stability in this awful moment.

Broken . . . broken. It wasn't possible. I knew that divorce across the nation was epidemic, and I was acutely aware of the tragic results of a broken home; but until now, until this very moment, I had thought of divorce as a misfortune that happened in other families, to other people. But now divorce was knocking on our door. This was *our* daughter, *our* grandchildren, *our* family.

I brought my thoughts back quickly. "Honey, why don't you come over and we'll talk. Dad will be home soon. Maybe we can help in some way."

"Maybe, mom." Her voice was small, uncertain.

We said goodbye. I stared at the receiver, reluctant to put it down, as though it somehow kept me in contact with my hurting daughter. I longed to be near her, to hold her close and assure her that all would be well. I strongly resisted the rising certainty that perhaps Nancy was right, perhaps Doug was gone for good.

Suddenly I longed for my husband, Vern, for the comfort of his presence, for the strength of his arms.

Instead, the steady hum of the air conditioner was my only companion; its noisy silence moved with me from room to room.

I waited through the lonely afternoon, reflecting sadly on love and marriage. Where does love go? Does it tiptoe out unsuspectingly amid dirty dishes, piled-up bills, batches of laundry, early morning feedings, grubby hands, chattering children? Or does it rush out like a torrent, dashing out the door in a blast of fury? Inanely, I thought about the death of love. Could it be buried, cremated, ashes thrown to the wind?

Doug, the tall, handsome young man who had courted our daughter through her teen years, had been like a fourth son. Throughout his high school days he had worked side by side with Vern. Watching them together, I had often breathed a prayer of thanksgiving that Nancy would be blessed with a husband much like my own—a kind, gentle man.

But during the past months, no, the past year, we had begun to notice subtle changes in their marriage, changes we neither wished to recognize nor to admit. We sensed that their lives were traveling in different directions; but I, not wishing to think the unthinkable, had refused to entertain such devastating thoughts.

Nancy must have kept her doubts locked silently and securely in her heart. Had her fears included the possibility that there might be another woman in Doug's life?

Questions tumbled about, only to be left unanswered—for who knew the answers but God alone, and didn't He caution us to live one day at a time, to trust our future to Him? How lovely this promise seemed when life was sailing smoothly; but how ethereal, how tenuous it seemed now. My fears would not be quelled.

Expecting Nancy's Volkswagen to pull into the driveway at any moment, I walked to the window; but the street outside was deserted. I paced the living room, trying to escape from my unpleasant thoughts. What would this mean to Nancy, to her sons, to Vern and me?

I called back the reassuring words I had just spoken to Nancy—perhaps this was only a temporary separation that would draw them closer together. Who knew? A time of testing, a time of healing, a time of reflection; and when they were reconciled, their love, their marriage, would become stronger, more secure.

Yes, I must believe, and convince Nancy to believe, too, that their marriage would be restored.

I had often encouraged others to look beyond their circumstances to God and to praise Him for what He would do. Now, sitting alone on this quiet afternoon, I was the one staring tragic circumstances straight in the face. I must relinquish this cold, gripping fear; I must resist all the frightening "what ifs" of tomorrow, I told myself. The God of tomorrow is the God of today. I must resolutely close the door of despair and open wide the gateway of hope. Whatever lies ahead, God has already been there; and although the road is unknown to us, it is familiar to Him. Could I trust with abandonment?

Like the murmur of the wind came a gentle promise from the comforting Psalms. ". . . don't be discouraged. Don't be upset. Expect God to act! For I know that I shall again have plenty of reason to praise him for all that he will do. He is my help! He is my God!" (Ps. 42:11 LB).

I took a deep breath and waited, quietly and without tears.

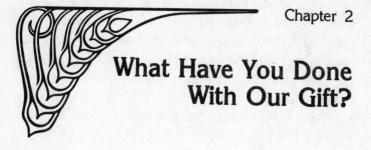

Chapter 2

What Have You Done With Our Gift?

I met Vern as he opened the door. Putting my arms around him, I tried to tell him what seemed too impossible to be true. As I cried and talked, he became thoughtful, his face reflecting a deep sadness.

"I think Doug will come back home once he's thought this over." He took my hand, but I felt he was simply trying to bolster my sagging spirits.

"Nancy said she would come over." I walked to the window again, peering into the dusky night. "They should have been here by now."

We sat in the den, side by side, waiting for the usual burst of noise that accompanied the arrival of our daughter and grandsons. None came, and the silence grew with the darkening shadows. I rose to change the television channel, snapped it off instead, and turned on the stereo, welcoming soft and soothing music into the quiet room.

Suddenly, in the strangest way, I remembered another night. Another night of waiting! The night of our daughter Kathi's accident. I had flown home from Northern California and was waiting on this very sofa, with Nancy beside me, for Vern and our sons to arrive home from Lake Shasta where we had been vacationing. The same heaviness I had experienced that night settled on me now. But why? Why should I be thinking about death? There had been no call from the Highway Patrol, no visit to the morgue, no preparations for a funeral, no mourning for a lost loved one. Like a shot into a nerve I discovered a painful truth that day. *Mourning is not reserved for death.*

The clock struck nine. Anger stirred within me. Where had Nancy gone for love and comfort? Now—now when her heartache must be at its apex, where had she gone? Why hadn't she come to us? How could she call, drop this shocking news into our lives, and disappear for the evening? The telephone at her home went unanswered. I glanced at Vern's face. His eyes were closed, his head back on the sofa. Suddenly I realized how painful this news must be for him. He had cared for Doug like a son. Was he wondering, as I was, how this unexpected turn would affect our lives? We both knew, of course, that our lives would change, but the shock of the immediate situation benevolently kept secret how greatly we would have to rearrange our comfortable way of life.

"Try not to worry, honey," I heard Vern saying to comfort me. "I'm sure Nancy went to a friend's house. She'll call us first thing in the morning."

I nodded absently, anger and hurt mingling with

tears. Why would she go to a friend's home—it was I, her mother, who had always rushed to apply whatever Band-Aid she ever needed.

My thoughts drifted to our family and friends. We would have to admit what seemed to be the failure of our children, as though we were accountable for their defeats. How true it is that our children's successes are the crown of our lives. How proud we always had been to recite their accomplishments, degrees, careers—all part of our dream.

We had prayed from the time Nancy was a baby for the man who would share her life. We had rejoiced at her wedding, for Doug seemed to be the perfect answer to that prayer. I had been filled with pleasure thinking of the joys that lay ahead for my daughter and her new husband. Now, ten years later, many of those joys had been fulfilled. They had a home of their own, two beautiful sons, Doug's successful career. Where, dear God, had the dream gone wrong?

Divorce seemed unthinkable! In my generation, anathema! Raised in the conservative Midwest as I had been, I became accustomed to how the divorced had been different, set apart. "They" did not participate in our churches as official leaders; and unless their divorce had been kept secret, they could rarely be educators. No, divorce was a spiritual as well as a social disgrace. Divorced individuals became an ignoble part of a fragmented society and were left to bear their stigma alone. And to remarry carried their disgrace to the limit—it was the ultimate transgression.

Even today, divorce left an unpalatable taste. "Oh no, dear God, I do not wish this for my daughter nor the term 'children of divorce' for my grandsons." Tears touched my lids, but I kept them securely locked between my lashes, trying to call up my former thoughts of hope and faith. They refused my bidding. I would come to know this pattern again and again in future days—the ambivalence of hope and despair. Like a door with double hinges, the winds of hope blew them one way one minute, and the winds of despair blew them the other direction the next minute.

Anger simmered toward Doug. How could he do this terrible thing? As I thought about it throughout that bitter evening, something close to hatred surfaced. Tears washed my face, but what I needed was something to soothe my aching heart. Just then, as though in answer to this unspoken plea, a picture flashed through my mind. I imagined Doug entangled in a net he had never expected to step into, his feet so entwined that he was trapped, unable to cut himself loose. The net had closed over him just as though he had stepped into a trap. I realized that this affair had probably begun innocently enough—a harmless friendship, perhaps. But such was the nature of traps.

In the days, months, and years ahead, that picture flashed back, erasing my fury and hatred. God, in His tender compassion, was asking me to show love and mercy toward this young man. I wept as wave after wave of sadness swept over me. I remembered their wedding day.

"Who gives this woman to this man?"

"Her mother and I do," Vern had responded in a clear, strong voice.

Remembering that beautiful evening and the joy I experienced as those two young people pledged lifelong vows to one another called up fresh tears.

The gift of love had been given. What had Doug done with our gift?

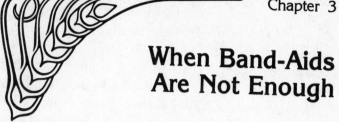

Chapter 3

When Band-Aids Are Not Enough

It was Monday evening before Nancy came with Josh and Kevin in hand, quietly subdued. She went through the motions of eating, pushing her food around the plate. When the boys went out to play, she began to talk nonstop, as though she had to speak the words aloud to believe the painful ordeal of the past days.

"I expected you to come here last night." I was still mildly upset over my fruitless, worried vigil.

"I know," Nancy said. "I know I should have called you again, but I hardly knew what I was doing. I dressed the boys, got into the car, and drove to the freeway. I passed station wagons filled with families, fathers driving . . ." She passed her hand over her eyes as though to blot out the memory. "Not me—it'll never be me again."

"But honey," I repeated, taking her cold hand, "why didn't you come here?"

"I'm sorry, mom. I didn't mean to worry you, but I went to a Sunday afternoon service. I took the boys to their class and sat in the back of the church. The first thing I heard was this verse:'The name of the Lord is a strong tower; the righteous shall run into it and be safe.'"

My eyes filled. Vern had been right. Nancy had gone to a friend's house. She had run straight to God. I, who had always been there providing mother love, could not fulfill her deepest need. She had been crying out for Holy Spirit comfort, the sureness of God's presence, and He had met her need.

"They served communion," she went on, "and we stood in a circle and prayed. I can't explain it, but the terrible scared feeling vanished. I renewed my commitment to follow the Lord, with or without Doug." She paused, then added thoughtfully, "I can't think about life without my husband—the boys without their daddy. I have to live one day at a time." She looked at us for reassurance, and we nodded.

I thought again about how parents relish their children's successes. How had we been measuring success? Had we been placing our greatest value on things, the world's yardstick for measuring prosperity? Wasn't it really faith that the Lord desired above all else?

Perhaps God brings us to the unexpected curves and twists in our road so we will come to "know Him, and fellowship with His suffering," so He can crown our lives with the genuine success of absolute trust and reliance on His faithfulness. Who cannot be happy with the American dream intact, surrounded by lush green grass and smooth waters? But in rocky places we grow to maturity; through suffering we begin to understand the pain of others.

I would not have chosen this sudden turn in our road, but it was chosen for me. My own faith would have to be stirred to believe that God was with us.

Nancy rose slowly from the table as darkness settled. I thought of her silent, empty house at the end of a winding dirt road and longed to keep her here. I yearned to hold our grandsons close to protect them from the inevitable difficulties that were to come.

We walked her to the car. With his arm around her shoulders, Vern told her to drive carefully.

"Don't tell the boys yet," he cautioned. "It's too soon. There's still hope that things will work out. Wait."

We watched her Volkswagen sputter away, turned, and walked slowly into the quietness of our home.

Long after midnight I was still awake. It was one of those times when feelings cannot be expressed, words cannot be found. I was on a down elevator, traveling to depths I did not wish to explore. I tried to read my Bible, but could not concentrate. Instead I stared at the maroon photo album on the bookshelf, the one I reserved for Nancy's family. Inside, carefully protected, were photos of happier times—Nancy's and Doug's wedding day, Doug's Navy days, their first home in a lovely new suburb, Nancy's pregnancies, their vacations, a smiling, happy couple holding first one then two baby boys. I continued to stare at the album, unable to open the pages, wishing it had been as easy to protect their relationship as it had been to protect those pictures. I placed it high on the top shelf, out of sight.

Sleep refused to befriend me. Was Nancy afraid at home alone? Would the sound of swaying trees keep her awake through the night? What if the boys became ill and she needed Doug? Where was he? Could she find him if she had to? My heart began to pound.

I painted a mental scenario. In the morning Doug would come, hold Nancy close, and they would renew their love. Yes, of course Vern was right, this was a phase. They needed to go to a marriage counselor, talk things out, learn to communicate. I knew of a psychologist in Long Beach and was confident he could see them through this stormy time.

Light began to stream through the windows, making me fitfully aware that I had not been able to hold back the dawn. I had not closed my eyes in sleep through the long night. I forced my weary body to relax and tried to concentrate.

"God is able to do immeasurably more than all we ask or imagine," I reminded myself. Certainly that could only mean that Doug and Nancy would be reconciled, for I would ask, and God would do.

Reason interrupted. God does not work against our wills. Life is a series of choices. We are given freedom, unlike puppets that are pulled and manipulated. In spite of faithful and earnest prayers, this separation might end in divorce.

Faith started, faltered, and sputtered like a failing engine. Divorce was heartache, rejection, scarred lives, a never-closed door where children were concerned.

I turned the ignition key once more. "God is our refuge and strength, an ever present help in trouble." Faith started this time—engine running smoothly. As the summer morning sunlight softly filtered into my bedroom, the majestic tenderness of the arms of God cradled me as I fell into a deep, sweet sleep.

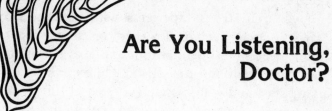

Chapter 4

Are You Listening, Doctor?

Nancy called the marriage counselor for an appointment, and the following day we made the long drive to Long Beach. My Monte Carlo sped along the freeway, the air conditioner mercifully keeping us cool. The smoggy skies held in the heat and shrouded the distant mountains into a faint outline.

I sat in the waiting room wondering where I had conceived the idea that anyone, expert in human behavior or not, could take the scrambled pieces of our lives, define them, and place them back again in perfect order.

In my vague consciousness I prayed that the counselor would give Nancy ten easy steps to restore her marriage and, until that wonderful day, that He would hold us all together.

Oh, foolish heart!

After the session, Nancy and I lunched on the deck of an old ship harbored on the blue Pacific. A light sea breeze rippled the waves, gently rocking the ship. What a delightful afternoon it would have been, if only—

Nancy relived her experience with the counselor. "He showed me a chart he called the Anatomy of an Affair," she said, "with graphs and charts and little lines that went up and down. He explained how affairs start and what a man experiences during this time. He said usually they cool within six to nine months. He said I should be patient and wait."

I tried to digest all this along with my alfalfa sprout sandwich.

"While he was explaining Doug's feelings, his experiences with this new girl, I felt like I was dying inside. I wanted to talk about how *I* felt, how hurt *I* was that he could leave me. I wanted to ask how long *I* should wait. Was my marriage over? What did I do to make him go to someone else? I needed him to tell me what to do. But he asked if I could lay my feelings aside and believe with him that this marriage could be healed." Her brown eyes were perplexed.

"Lay your feelings aside?" I too was puzzled. "But it seems to me that you must express how you feel, talk about your hurt and anger, explain your confusion in order to resolve how you feel."

"So it seemed to me!" In spite of all the tension she had been through, Nancy began to laugh. "The doctor did say there is one of two things that will happen: either Doug will come home, or he'll stay with his girlfriend."

We looked at each other and burst into laughter. One hour's drive and forty-five dollars later and she was at square one.

"Do you want to know what his big suggestion was?" She smiled again, though there was pain in her eyes. "He said I should go to the beach with Doug and the boys and play frisbee. *Frisbee!*"

I conjured up the picture of Nancy on the beach throwing the brightly colored disc through the air, Doug playfully catching it, and the boys racing happily between them.

It was a lovely family scene, only something was wrong with the picture. Nancy wasn't the girl at the beach.

"How can I play frisbee with a disappearing husband?" Nancy rested her chin in her hand and gazed over the ocean at swooping gulls. A tear slid down her cheek.

"Do you want to know what I'm doing while they're at the beach? I'm lying on my kingsize bed in the suffocating heat counting flowers marching up the wallpaper. Do you know there are exactly fifty-four daisies in each row? I lie on the bed and stare at the wall, wondering how my perfect life could have come to this place."

"Nancy," I touched her arm, "maybe you should see the counselor one more time. One visit doesn't seem enough of an indicator of what he might be able to offer."

She nodded. "I already made another appointment."

On the drive home we talked of Josh and Kevin, of their questions, of what she should tell them, of what words she should use.

"This morning," she said sadly, "I heard Kevin's

little voice talking to himself. 'Yup,' he said, 'there's only one person in mom's bed.'"

What must he be thinking? My heart took a dive.

"He's been waking in the night crying for daddy. And Josh has been wanting to know where he is, why he can't call him. I have to know what to tell them—soon."

The next week we made the second trip to the marriage counselor. Another disappointment. On the drive home Nancy was verbally angry.

"He didn't listen to me, to my inner feelings. He kept trying to explain how Doug must be experiencing these new and wonderful feelings. Well . . ." She paused and gazed out the window at the passing landscape. "I'm not willing to play 'wait and see' games. I need help for *me*, now."

I stayed at her home that night until after the boys were asleep. We sat at her table, sipped herbal tea, and talked about God's faithfulness and timing, how we are cautioned to wait on the Lord—not on Doug, not on circumstances, not on words of wisdom from a marriage counselor—but on the Lord. We agreed that waiting is one of the most difficult things to do, but that we must remember God's perspective is eternal, His time unlimited, and that His purpose is to conform and mold us into the image of Christ.

Close to midnight, when I got up to leave, Nancy handed me a paper from her daily journal. I slipped it into my purse.

Circling my car around the cul-de-sac, I began the long drive down the winding road. I recalled a phrase I had read that morning in *My Utmost for His Highest*. "If God has made your cup sweet, drink it with grace; if He has made it bitter, drink it in communion with Him."

Many times in my life the Lord had required that I drink bitter water in communion with Him, some of it bitter beyond belief. And yet, even the most bitter had become sweet in His time.

I pulled into our driveway with one thought in mind—crawling into my kingsize bed, falling soundly asleep, and allowing the memories of the day to fall into oblivion. But I remembered the paper Nancy had handed me and I sat down at the kitchen table to read what she had written.

Tears fell as I read her heart's cry:

Here I Am Alone, Lord

It's evening, the house is dark, and the children are sleeping peacefully
In their land of childhood dreams,
Securely content.

The doorbell has ceased its maddening echo, beckoning my little ones
To come out and play.

It's late, too late for even the closest of friends to call;
The quiet is soothing after a hectic nonstop day.

And now I am alone.
Small adventures filled my day.
Stimulating classes forced hurting thoughts from my mind.
An hour of noisy cookie baking, little fingers dipping gingerly

Into honey-raisin batter.
Shining faces impatient for warm cookies to melt onto outstretched hands.
My day was full, but now I am alone.

I long to share today, the scattered portions of my life,
Etching out my identity for someone close to look and see who I am.
I took it so for granted, Lord, the ease of married love,
Someone close to share thoughts of our crowded days.

I don't like living alone, Lord.
It seems as though this world was made for twos.
We were Mr. and Mrs., together forever, I never once doubted that.
I was like a computer with no card punched 'divorce'.
Never was there the tiniest space in my mind that he would
Walk away and leave us behind.

But now I am alone, Lord.
I didn't wish for it, nor did I foresee this heartbreak road, nor
Do I understand why I must walk this way at all.
But now, even now, as I share my thoughts with You on this quiet night,
I know Your presence and peace are here.

You quietly remind me that You understand loneliness.
You wept alone in the garden while Your closest friends slept.
You know about rejection, Lord.
You were so alone for that awful forsaken time on the cross.
I will never, ever be that alone.

You know my deepest suffering, my broken dreams, my silent hurts.
You know the wonder in my children's faces
At the empty place their daddy left behind.
Your Father arms are underneath, gently protecting.
Oh, Lord, Father us.
As sleep carries me into another world, stand guard at my dreams, Lord,
Set my inner meditations to praise
So that when I awaken, it will be to a morning of joy.

Chapter 5

Daddy, Please Come Home

How one can function in the midst of trauma and paroxysms of grief is difficult to understand, but the flow of life must go on. Children must be dressed and fed, clothes washed and folded, groceries purchased and put away, hair cut and styled. Life does not stand still for tragedy or change or happiness or joy.

The time came when the children needed to be told. Their inquiring minds were begging for answers.

"Josh asked again this week why daddy wasn't coming home," Nancy told me over our weekly lunch. "I continued to water the plants, trying to think of something he would understand, but I couldn't. Not then. But that night after Kevin was asleep, Josh and I were sitting on the sofa together, and I asked him, 'Josh, do you understand about falling in love?'"

"'Yeah,' he said, but he wouldn't look at me.

"'Well,' I told him, 'dad's fallen in love with

someone else. You know Joanna?' He stared at me, his eyes wide. I knew he half understood, but couldn't comprehend what this would mean to him. Then I asked, 'Josh, do you know about divorce?' He said he knew about divorce because Kenny's parents were divorced and Nathan's and Christy's. He whispered, 'Mom, who will take care of us?'"

We were silent. I couldn't have spoken a word at that moment if I had wanted to. I knew when Nancy told Josh she had been on a swaying bridge, fearful that one wrong step might cause a devastating fall.

"I explained to him," Nancy turned her cup around and around in the saucer, tears standing in her eyes, "that God would take care of us, and that dad would give us money so we could stay in our house. I told him that sometimes grownups can't live together. He cuddled up to me and was so quiet. Then I felt his shoulders shaking. I held him close and we cried together. But at last it's out in the open. What a terribly heavy burden to lay on a little boy."

"On two little boys," I thought aloud. Surely Kevin, so precocious, would have to be told soon.

After I promised her Vern and I would take the boys for the weekend, we finished our lunch and parted. Now that they knew the truth, I somehow felt it was our responsibility to make up for the loss.

In looking back on those frequent weekends that we kept Josh and Kevin, I smile, thinking how we tried to fill the empty space by "doing or buying."

I remember the first time we entered the noisy

child-filled room of the pizza parlor. I nearly bolted. What a place to be on a Friday night. How distantly removed from our usual dining in plush restaurants with friends, enjoying adult conversation bereft of interrupting small voices. Sitting at a benchlike table, root beer pitcher centering the table, pizza covering our plates, I gazed about at children crowded into booths with their young parents, rock music blaring, computer games flashing, kids queuing up to feed their precious quarters into the hungry machines.

I met Vern's eyes. If I hadn't laughed I would have cried. What were we doing here and why had our lives suddenly reversed? Why these steps back in time? How long would it be before our lives were back to normal?

I also remember the torridly hot August afternoon we took them to Disneyland. We stood under the blazing sun in perpetually long lines, rode on boats through cool damp caverns, thrilled with them to "It's a Small World," and stayed until dusk to watch the Mickey Mouse parade. It was a wonderful day for them, but we couldn't provide them with a forever Disneyland. Life was not a fanciful adventure, a weekend wonderland. Monday morning reality was always just ahead.

And the reality of one particular Monday morning was almost more than I could bear. Forever etched on the calendar of my mind is the day I found Josh's note. I had seen him the night before, bent over my desk, intently printing on a piece of paper. The next morning, after he had gone home, I found it—a note to his father. I read the large childish printing.

> *Daddy, please come home. I want you to come home. Kevin and I want you to come home. We'll be good. Please come home. Love from Josh and Kevin.*

I carried Josh's note with me from room to room, failing in my effort to hold back tears. They streamed down my face as I prayed and walked the floor.

> *Lord, please, please restore this family. Dear, sweet Jesus, you promised if I asked anything in Your name You would do it. This is my anything. Keep this little family together.*

I desperately needed someone to talk to, someone outside our family who could relate and listen. I dialed the number of a friend and told her about Nancy's separation, of Josh's plea to his daddy, explaining that I felt so helpless and depressed. But during that call something happened. Though she did not say so in words, it became apparent that she did not wish to become involved in this so private a grief. She subtly switched the conversation to more pleasant topics. I hung up the receiver numbly. Had I been wrong to hope that someone would listen and maybe say so simply, "I can't understand what you are feeling, but I do love you now."

Resentment stirred toward my friend. But I slowly realized how many times I had been guilty of the same thing—of not allowing my spirit to touch the spirit of another and to truly enter into his or her

suffering. Perhaps this painful experience would remind me in the future that often the only words a
hurting person needs to hear are "I care about
you . . . I love you."

When I showed Josh's note to Vern that evening, a
look of despair clouded his face. I could sense he had
come to the place where he needed to do something.
He went to the telephone to call Doug for the first
time since the separation. Doug agreed to come by
and talk with us the following evening; and he did.

As I watched Doug sitting uneasily on our sofa, I
felt detached, like a person witnessing an unfolding
drama who knows all along how the plot will end.

"I hope you both understand how sorry I am," he
said. "I still love Nancy and the boys, but I've
changed. I'm a different person now."

I mentally agreed. I could see that he was different and that he had been changing for some time.

Vern talked of Josh and Kevin and of the
heartbreaking consequences for them of being raised
in a fatherless home. Doug listened carefully, nod-
ding in agreement, but there was no question that he
had made an irrevocable decision. He actually
seemed puzzled that we could not understand why
he had to leave his family. A car pulled up to our
curb, and Doug stood up. It was Joanna. Doug
shook hands with Vern as though a business trans-
action had been completed and hugged me, whispering, "I'm sorry." I felt sure that he was, but it
didn't relieve the helpless, foreboding feeling I had.
We handed him Josh's note, and he slipped it into
his pocket.

No, Joshua, Daddy will not be coming home!

I had been warned by my divorced friends that their children's emotions were often expressed in subtle, unexpected ways. Our grandsons were no exception.

One Sunday after church, Vern and I were walking back to the car holding hands with Josh and Kevin. Kevin skipped.

"Now, we're a family," he beamed.

On the drive home I asked, "What do you think a family is, Kevin?"

"Well," his brown eyes looked straight into mine, "families are together and they love each other."

He *knew!* Somehow, though he had never been told in so many words, he knew his family as he had known it was dissolved. My heart plunged.

I wondered if he felt abandoned. Born a happy, smiling child, he had been whining recently and crying for his mother's attention. Did he fear that if one parent left, the other might also leave?

After dinner, while I read to him from his favorite storybook, he suddenly interrupted. "I want my daddy. I don't want to see him just on Sundays. I want him in my own house every day. I wish," he sobbed, "I wish the phone had arms and I could call him and he could hug me right through the phone."

I rocked him gently, thinking how true it is that when a certain pair of arms are needed no one else's arms will do.

Kevin's agonized plea uncovered all my carefully hidden anger toward Doug; but I knew I must comfort Kevin without saying a word against his father. Doug was still an important part of his life—his heritage—and Kevin needed to know his father, whom he loved, was a good person. Though my anger begged to be verbalized, judging Doug was not my responsibility and it certainly wouldn't help Kevin.

Kevin was still sobbing, "What if you and grandpa break?" he asked.

I closed the book and set him on my lap. "We won't, Kev," I promised, looking into his puzzled eyes.

"But how do you know?" His lip was trembling. I held him closely, thinking back over our thirty-plus-year marriage—of our good and difficult places, of unhappy surprises, of noisy, confusing years raising five children. There was no doubt in my mind that Vern and I had been held together by the stubborn hand of God, securely in His grip. He had been the cohesive force in our lives. If one of us had let go of Him, we would have broken.

I rocked Kevin gently, whispering into his honey-colored hair.

"We won't break, Kev. I'm so sorry mommy and daddy did, but darling . . . they'll always love you and be there for you and . . ."

I groped for brilliant words of wisdom that would reinforce his shaken world, but instead I broke down and began to cry. Together, although generations apart, Kevin and I held each other and wept.

Chapter 6

Friends and Comforters

Life was never meant to be a lonely journey. If ever friendship was urgently needed it was now, not only by Nancy, but by us, her parents. During that first year, I longed for someone who would fulfill the biblical command to weep with those who weep. I desperately needed someone to weep with me. I remembered the many friends who had poured into our home after Kathi's death. They had wept freely with us then, where were they now? Death, I began to realize, has no stigma attached to it. It is not a threat to the Christian community. But divorce is. To Christians, death, though extremely painful, represents a kind of victory. Divorce represents failure.

Once when I was relating my feelings to a friend, tears filled her eyes. Gratitude that she cared enough to share my sorrow in a visible way warmed my heart. I needed her tears, her expression of love and understanding. I shall never forget those precious few who understood the path we had fallen on;

usually they were the ones who had traveled the same road before us.

Regretfully, however, most did not understand, even our longtime friends. One afternoon following a delightful conversation with a Christian friend at a bridal shower, she politely asked about my family. I explained to her that Nancy was separated and probably would be divorced. Her friendly attitude changed immediately, and she waved her hand in a gesture of disapproval. "Don't talk to me about divorce," she protested. "I don't believe in it." Thus ended our social chat.

Alone that evening, I wept bitterly, well aware that at one time my own reaction would have been very similar. Although I might not have said it, I probably would have thought that if the couple had only been committed Christians, had read the Bible and prayed together, and had attended church faithfully, the divorce could have been avoided. And indeed, those things may have kept them together, but what if one resisted? And who was I, sitting on my lofty perch with other happily married couples, to make that generalization?

I slowly began to understand it was not that these particular friends *would* not offer understanding, but that they *could* not. I recalled times when I had made awkward attempts at conversations, not knowing what to say.

Years before, Vern and I had sponsored a class of single adults. In spite of our efforts to reach them, however, there was a definite barrier. We had spent much time with them and opened our home for weekend socials, but nothing seemed to work. I finally understood why when Charlotte, a pretty divorcee, said to me angrily, "How could *you* understand? How could you possibly know what we are facing?"

She was right. I could not understand her heartache and rejection and her desperation over trying to support and raise three children. I had never traveled that road.

Now, however, our own daughter was suddenly single, and because I, like most parents, am but a minute away from my children's pain, I could look back on those young singles and see why I had been unable to offer anything other than superficiality. True, we had stretched ourselves to the best of our ability; but knowing what I know now, I would have taken a different view. Back in those safe and happy days it was easy to give pat answers, to walk away from heartache, and to join our own couples' crowd, forgetting there was another world out there.

Perhaps God was allowing this journey so that in the future we would better understand how to comfort lonely hearts.

Nancy's life widened, and for that I was grateful. Friends poured affection into her lonely places. Kids she had counseled at camp came to her home, pizzas in hand, sensing that their presence was a gift they could offer. They sat on her family room floor chatting away the hours and offered to babysit whenever needed. Three young college boys came one Saturday, paint brushes in hand, and redecorated her home. With freshly painted walls and a bright floral sofa in her family room, Nancy's spirits lifted. I breathed a sigh of relief when the wallpaper with the climbing daisies was replaced by a tiny floral print in baby blue.

God had not abandoned Nancy in a friendless ocean. He had provided lifelines—all in the form of His children.

Our three sons called her often and took her to dinner. They who had once been the "little brothers" for whom she babysat, now towered over her and became the support system she so desperately needed. How the cycle had changed. We were especially amazed by our middle son, Dave, who had just turned twenty-one. The night I told him that Doug had left Nancy he said quietly, "I know. I've seen it coming. I may have to help raise those boys." In the years to come, I realized that Dave had not spoken idle words. Many times I saw him bending over the table helping the boys with their homework, driving them for ice cream, decorating their house for Christmas. He rode bikes with them, taught them to throw and catch a ball, attended their soccer games each Saturday, and disciplined them when it was necessary. I marveled that our young son had the insight to know how much those little boys needed a strong male role model. But Dave's insight did not end with the boys. He also sensed what his sister needed. He stepped into the center of her life and became her rock of steadiness. His tender, compassionate nature helped him understand her pain. He made the trip to her home three or four times a week and called each evening to see if everything was OK.

In contrast to family and friends who became an umbrella of love for Nancy, however, were the many "Job's comforters" who did not hesitate to offer their counsel. They knew why this had happened, what she must or must not do, and what God intended to teach her through this trial. Some even took advantage of her vulnerability and need for fellowship by inviting her to their homes, only to quote well-rehearsed phrases about how much God hates divorce. One middle-aged couple in particular, during the height of her apprehension, warned her that she must never, ever initiate divorce proceedings—that she must wait prayerfully and patiently for Doug to return home.

Anger simmered inside me when she called to tell me about their immovable stance and the fear they had instilled in her.

"What did you say to them?" I asked, forcing back my inner rage.

"I asked them why Jesus permitted divorce for unfaithfulness. They said that was for the hardness of their hearts. You wouldn't want that said of you, would you?"

They had found her vulnerability: guilt. Of course she wouldn't want that said of her.

Discouragement poured from her voice. "They told me I must never divorce Doug because God would have to chasten me if I did. They pointed to June Nielson. She has waited for five years. What they don't know is that June's husband is about to remarry."

"Mom," Nancy went on, "they listed twenty-three things that could happen if I should file for divorce."

The phrase "God hates divorce" sang a haunting tune. It was true. He did. And so did we.

Nancy was desperate to know where her life was heading and what, if anything, she should do. Her emotions sailed on ambivalent waves. She hated Doug. She loved Doug. She never wanted to see him again. She wanted him back under any circumstance. The boys needed their father. She didn't want them to see him again. Up and down and around her unsettled thoughts traveled. Surely, somewhere, there must be a servant of God who would listen and offer godly direction for this uncharted voyage.

And so it was that such a man entered our lives at the precise moment of need.

Chapter 7

"And Now He Has"

Dr. Dallas Willard, professor of philosophy at the University of Southern California, was the man God sent to settle our stormy seas. Although he had earned many degrees and had translated scholarly textbooks into various languages, it was his simplicity and godly spirit that captured our attention when he first spoke at our church. His message that day on the Sermon on the Mount seemed to be delivered directly to our hearts and lives for that time.

He believed that when Jesus spoke of divorce in Matthew 5 He was speaking to a culture in which women were totally dependent on men for everything. They had no identity apart from their husbands.

Dr. Willard further explained that the whole point of the Sermon on the Mount was to correct the erroneous teaching of Jesus' day—that one could obtain righteousness by keeping the law. Jesus was revealing the futility of that belief. But for some reason, when it comes to divorce, Dr. Willard pointed

49

out, Christian leaders still try to make everyone "keep the law." He went on to explain what a contradiction that is because we don't call ourselves murderers because we have been angry, nor adulterers because we have lusted; but we insist on calling remarried divorced people adulterers.

Dr. Willard closed his Bible quoting the words of Jesus, "Therefore you are to be perfect, as your Heavenly Father is perfect."

A chilling command. How could this be possible? Who could be perfect but God alone?

As Dr. Willard prayed, tears poked through my eyelids. Questions stirred in my mind, and I determined that we must meet this man for an intimate conversation. He might be the one to counsel our distraught daughter.

Vern and I drove home in silence, but our thoughts were probably very similar. We had been raised with the identical teaching Dr. Willard had spoken about—that there are certain "rules" Christians must keep. These rules are invisibly numbered according to their importance, so Christians can keep track of how righteous they are before God. I recalled my teenage years. I had been led to believe that my overall outward appearance, and what I did or did not do determined my spirituality, rather than my inner motives and who I already was in Christ.

And, of course, I was taught that divorce was high on the scale of absolute no-nos. And remarriage, even for the unfortunate innocent party, was out of the question. Although we were taught that God's gift of salvation was freely given and although we sang verse after verse of "Amazing Grace," we proceeded to pay close attention to our rule-keeping.

After Vern and I were married, we still accepted many of those values; but as we matured in the faith and moved away from such a legalistic environment, we found a fresh freedom that helped us recognize that our intricately designed maze of traditional beliefs was not God's design at all.

In California Vern served on various deacon boards and suffered through long discussions concerning the divorced. He began to push aside the cobwebs of manmade rules and gently raised the issue of the greatest commandment of all—love. Angry board members denounced the divorced, raising difficult questions at each meeting. Could "they" serve in an official capacity? Would the pastor remarry a divorced person? Could "they" become church members? Sing in the choir? Iron bars steeled these "second-class Christians" from full fellowship and service.

Many times Vern stood alone. Sin was sin, he insisted. God hated all sin, yet loved sinners and received them with open arms. So certainly He hated the sin of pride as much as He hated divorce. After all, Jesus denounced the religious leaders of His day for their self-righteousness. Were we any different? What a web of confusion we Christians had woven around ourselves concerning this volatile subject. Viewpoints varied: divorce was never permissible, no matter what the circumstances were; divorce was permissible for "biblical" reasons; di-

vorce was permissible, but remarriage was not; remarriage was permissible, but there could be no
official wedding ceremony in the church.

My thoughts focused on Nancy again. Even
though she had been an unwilling party to a separation, she would face spiritual and emotional suffering, set apart from the mainstream of Christianity.
Yet, thanks to Dr. Willard, we had seen this moun-
tain of suffering from a new perspective, and its
rough edges of grief had been smoothed.

We invited Dr. Willard and his wife, Jane, to our
home to meet Nancy. We told them of our concern
for her and briefly explained about the people telling
her she must wait for Doug, even if it took forever.
His wife, we discovered, was a marriage counselor
who was willing to share her own experiences and
insights. Their friendship was to fill a unique place
in our lives during the time we were so needy.

Dr. Willard agreed to talk with Nancy, and when
he and his wife came the following Sunday evening,
they invited Vern and me to join them around the
fireplace in the living room. Outside, a gentle rain
played a quiet melody in concert with the blazing
fire. Nancy sat on the floor, her face a mask of tension and strain.

First, Dr. Willard leaned forward and asked
Nancy to share her feelings. She spoke slowly and
thoughtfully of the past months, of her hurt and
rejection, of her life that she felt was shattered like
glass, broken around her feet, the pieces too tiny to
touch. She told him about the weariness that drag-
ged her spirits down, how she often felt too heavily

laden to even get out of bed. Thinking ahead to raising her sons alone, she wondered how she would support them. Questions that had oppressed and confused her poured from her heart. She spoke of the previous year, how she had wondered why she and Doug were drifting apart, and how she blamed herself for trying to make Doug over, for wanting him to become someone he didn't wish to be. She talked of all the "I should have dones" and "I should have beens." She related how she could relax in trust one day and then feel sudden fear running through her like the chill of an icy wind the next. Shock, bewilderment, and guilt kept pointing to her as the failure. She relived the past year until dusk shadowed the window and the flames in the fireplace burned low.

At last she told of the couple who had invited her to their home and who had listed all the things that would happen should she proceed with divorce. Like a prison warden handcuffing a convict, they had bound her tightly with what they believed to be undeniable facts, and Nancy could not escape.

When she finished, she gazed into the fireplace, her face motionless.

After a short silence, Dr. Willard asked, "What are these 'things' this couple listed for you, Nancy?"

She continued to stare at the burning logs. "Well, in essence they said that I must never divorce Doug because it would be an act of defiance. I would be out from under his protection and would open myself up to attacks by Satan. They said my children would not have a godly upbringing and that if I remarried I would be committing adultery and would establish a pattern of adultery in the family. They warned that I would deny my children the privilege of seeing me suffer."

"You see, Nancy," Dr. Willard began to explain, "these 'things' they say will happen are the result of a system that defines rules-keeping as righteousness. For instance, according to them, if you do what they believe the Bible says is right, then whatever happens will not be your fault. So, if you wish to avoid blame, you must keep their list of rules. Sometimes well-meaning people make up rules and invite us to keep them. If we do, we become righteous; and because we are righteous, God will take care of us. This is really a doctrine of works, no matter how much grace is spoken over it."

Then Dr. Willard explained some of the things to Nancy that had meant so much to Vern and me when we had first heard him preach.

"Jesus' teachings concerning particular areas of life were given to correct erroneous general ideas and practices prevalent at that time," he continued. "When he taught that the poor would inherit the earth and that those who loved God must also love their enemies, the religious leaders thought He was crazy. Those concepts were foreign to their way of thinking. They considered the rich to be high on heaven's list of 'who's who.'

"What many Christians today fail to understand is that Jesus' teaching concerning divorce was spoken to a particular audience, at a particular time, for a particular reason. In His day, if a woman was divorced by her husband, she lost her home, her children, and her honor. Most alternatives involved complete degradation of her spirit. Were she to marry again, she would be counted as used merchandise. If her parents did consent to receive her back into their home, she would be more of a servant than a daughter, for she had brought disgrace on their name. About the only other alternative was prostitution. In light of *that* culture, Jesus warned men not to put away their wives.

"Besides," Dr. Willard went on, "if we are to take the teachings of Jesus as an absolute law of righteousness, to be consistent we must follow everything He said to the letter. For instance, Jesus told His disciples to wash one another's feet. Some Christians do this with deep convictions; others declare this is not a literal teaching and follow their own cultural background. But Jesus said we are to do as He did, and He washed His disciples' feet. Also, Jesus' teachings against anger, going to court against a fellow believer, swearing, and lusting were just as strong as His teaching against divorce. But do Christians make the penalty for these sins the same as for divorce? No.

"We must not be inconsistent and declare that some passages from the Sermon on the Mount are not applicable for the church age but others are. Using the Bible like that only serves our own petty prejudices.

"It is easy for those who are not involved in a divorce to look down on those who are and say 'it should never be' without ever looking into the circumstances. Many women have been threatened and beaten and are fearful for their lives. Yet they are warned they must make the best of the situation. Women have endured humiliation and sexual and emotional starvation because of the misinterpretation of Jesus' statement. It has been used as a key to lock us in the iron cage of law rather than to open the lock and set us free, as it was intended to do.

"God is working in your life, Nancy," Dr. Willard assured her, "to conform you to His image. And He's working in Doug's life and in your children's lives, and the important thing for you to do is accept Christ's love and learn to live His life in the middle of all these trials and heartaches."

Nancy's voice was small when she finally spoke. "Then should I file for divorce? Are all those 'things'? . . ."

"That is a decision that must be made between you and God. I could suggest that you set a date and tell Doug that on that day he must come to a decision."

"He won't. He wants me to file for divorce, but I'd rather not . . ." Her voice trailed away.

Dr. Willard spoke gently. "Of course, I don't blame you for not wanting to file. If that fear is deep enough, it might be better for you to wait. You must come to grips with what God is telling you, and if you have any uncertainties, then wait. And if it is worth it to you to favor your friends, if it would help them in some way, then wait."

"It's hard to think of divorce because of the children." Nancy's eyes yielded to sudden tears. "Just this morning, Josh said, 'Mom, do you love dad?' I said, 'Yes, I do, Josh.' Then he asked, 'Then why are we getting a divorce? If you and dad don't divorce, he'll come home to us.'"

"You must be very honest with your children," Dr. Willard warned. "They can handle truth. What they cannot handle are guesses and misinterpretations and wondering. Tell them that you love them, that their dad loves them, and that you are as unhappy as they are. I believe Doug has feelings for you, Nancy, and I believe he wants to be tender and do what's right for you and the boys."

"But that's not a commitment," Nancy replied softly.

"No, it's not. But he's unsure of himself. You must spend much time in prayer, waiting for the Lord to make things clear to you before you make any final determination. Since you have not been one to make decisions, it will be difficult for you. Many times women are told to let their husbands do the decision-making. That's fine—until the decision-maker disappears."

What comfort that evening brought—to Vern and me as well as to Nancy. The questions that had lingered in her eyes seemed to vanish, and the tension left her face as though an invisible cord had been cut.

Dr. Willard had not offered pat answers, light promises, or frothy advice about manipulating one's mate. Even my own thoughts were untangling as I dwelt on God that evening, on His mercy and grace, on His Fatherhood, and on His sure guidance to His own children.

Once during the evening as Nancy sat gazing into the fire, she had voiced her inner thoughts, her sentences halting, as though she were talking to herself.

"The past year has been unhappy for both of us," she said. "We couldn't really talk to each other. We should have gotten help sooner; yet our paths took different turns before we could realize what was happening. Many things happened that only Doug and I know about. I know he loved me and still loves me in a way, and I'll always love the boy I married. I could have done many things differently. I must have seemed self-righteous to him in many ways. It was inevitable that he would find someone more compatible with his new lifestyle. I probably never would have left him. But one night after a particularly bad time, I drove my car around and around in a rainstorm, crying out to God to please deliver me from the pain of our dying relationship."

Dr. Willard turned, looked intently at Nancy, and softly spoke the words that settled her troubled heart, "And now He has."

Chapter 8

Shattered Dreams

Thanksgiving brought our family together for the usual turkey feast. And, as holidays have a way of doing, it revealed the changes in our family as nothing else could have. Perhaps because we want everything to stay the same, we notice changes more acutely at family gatherings. This year was especially different, not only because Doug was not present, but because we had invited a young couple to be our guests for the day. They were newly settled in California, and we thought they might enjoy sharing this special day with a family; but it was a mistake for Nancy. They were about her age and had been married the same ten years, but their faces glowed with in-love happiness. Nancy was unable to make conversation, her face pale, her usual vibrancy vanished. I was glad to see the day end.

That night after our company had left, Nancy mentioned to me something her pastor had told her when he first heard about the separation. "When the time comes that you must sever your relationship with Doug legally," he had counseled, "you will know in your heart and nothing will shake it."

Ironically, that unshakable feeling came just after an unusually close moment between Nancy and Doug. A few days after Thanksgiving, Nancy became feverishly ill. Doug stopped by, sat on the edge of the bed, held her hand, laid a cool cloth on her forehead, and spoke gently.

"As he sat there," she told me later, "I felt love between us, a chance for our first love to be reborn. He was gentle, and I wanted him to hold me and tell me he loved me. But the moment passed, and before I could think how it happened, we were discussing property settlement."

Without her saying so, I knew that the unshakable feeling had settled her heart. She realized the twin-hinged door must be closed, and that she must be the one to close it. Though she had suspected from the beginning that there would be no reconciliation, now all doubt vanished. She wrote in her journal a heartbreaking expression of the world that had crashed about her.

*Lord, what do I do with these shattered dreams I hold
In my hand?
Do I discard them like old broken glass, or do I hold on a
little longer?
My mind cannot comprehend how a person who promised
me
Forever love can simply walk away.
Do ten years count for nothing? When I open my hand
and*

Look at the shattered dreams, I weep.

Life was an excursion for us, raising children, buying our

First home, taking trips. We had a million dreams for the future.

Lord, what do I do now?

Sometimes I wonder just exactly how love dies,

Because with the death of love, dreams die, too.

If I continue to hold these shattered fragments that once

Were our dreams, I'm afraid they will only cut my hand

And cause more pain.

Lord, you said you want to take our shattered dreams;

But You know I'm not strong enough to throw them away.

And, Lord, I'm afraid to live without dreams.

Here . . . take them from me as I open my hand and offer them to You.

Now I stand empty-handed. Please pour Your healing power

Through me and give me hope for the future.

The following day at her home Nancy told me sadly but firmly, "Mom, it's time—it's time to file for divorce. I must get on with my life." Her jaw was firm as she told me exactly when she would file the papers.

A year had gone by. A year of shock, anger, denial, and now acceptance. The exact stages of mourning a death.

There would be no more wondering and hoping that their love would be rekindled. The tiniest spark had been extinguished when they discussed property settlement.

On the familiar winding road back home I wept. As I wiped the tears from my cheeks, I knew they were different than the myriad I had shed before. They flowed with a sad finality, for I, too, had entered the stage of acceptance. Finally, they were tears of relief.

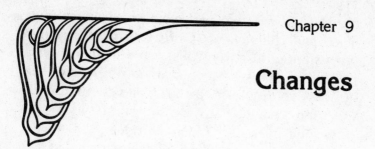

Chapter 9

Changes

Early in December Dave packed his clothes and his beloved books and moved into his sister's spare room. Yes, he said, he realized the long drive into college every day would be tedious, but Josh and Kevin needed him; it was something he had to do.

"No one should get married and have kids until they've lived with a family for a while," he joked a few weeks later. We laughingly agreed. Despite the joy children bring to our lives, they are often noisy, unruly, and disobedient. Although Josh and Kevin were no exception, Dave made the best of the situation. I marveled at his ability to make them obey and at how much the boys adored him. He became a security lock to the family.

One chilly night a week before Christmas, Dave took Josh and Kevin to a vast lot to choose a Christmas tree. With Kev high on Dave's shoulders, he and Josh walked slowly between row after row of tall evergreens. Patiently, Dave allowed the boys to point to this tree or that tree as the perfect one. At

63

last they discovered a perfectly formed six-foot pine. The wonderful scent of a Christmas tree always stirs up memories. Some of this year's memories were painful, but Dave's presence and love blotted them out. As we decorated the tree and the house, we wouldn't be singing any sad songs.

Looking over the family table loaded with our traditional Christmas Eve buffet, I marveled at how many changes had crisscrossed our lives. Kathi's place, once vibrant, was now empty. Doug was absent. Our three sons, once small boys, were now grown men. And we had encouraged Nancy to invite friends for dinner, so four college men from UCLA joined us at the table to feast and celebrate this most holy season.

After our guests were gone and the family was asleep, I walked through the living room, absently stacking toys and gifts under the tree, cleaning away the debris of opened gifts. Our Christmas Eve celebration was over, marking the end of our holiday crescendo. I sat down in my favorite chair, gazed into the glowing embers of the fireplace, and considered what the New Year might bring.

Within a week this year would come to an end. I, for one, was happy to say goodbye. We had been surprised by unexpected detours, tears, separation, unhappiness, spiritual awakenings, promises asked, answers given. Surely the New Year would bring a promise of renewal. I loved new things—polished, bright, shining things. Even as a child I had tiptoed my way into the New Year as though a miracle of new things would appear at the moment the midnight bells sounded. Pealing chimes change nothing, of course, but the child within me expected each New Year to bring exciting beginnings.

One beginning in particular I knew was imperative. Nancy must begin to study full time to finish college. She had taken a few classes the year before toward her goal of teaching health-science, but now she must accelerate her pace. Her most basic need in the years to come would be the ability to support herself and her sons.

The options seemed so few. No matter how I tried to ignore the fact, there seemed only one feasible path. I would have to step back into my long-deserted role as a secretary. For the past nine years I had been writing and speaking and immensely enjoying the niche I had found. Thinking ahead to the confines of a daily routine and regular office hours sent my spinning mind into a weary prayer.

Dear Lord, if ever I needed Your strength and wisdom it's now. I am helpless, and the road ahead does not look pleasant. Help me remember that I can only see things as they look outwardly. Whatever it is you have planned, give me a willing heart. Instill within me the belief that great good will come from this present pain. Help me know that it isn't important for me to understand why our road has turned so sharply, but to know that You have walked there before us. That is all I need to understand. Amen.

Chapter 10

Tag, You're It

After nearly a decade, I was back in an office as a *temporary* secretary. I could not bring myself to commit to a full-time job. All around me, however, were divorced women who were not only working full time, but who were struggling to raise their children alone as well. As I witnessed their dilemma, my decision to help our daughter finish her degree was reinforced.

One day Nancy called the office. "Mom," her voice sounded faint, "I'm sick."

Dave was in classes and staying at our house for the week to cram for his finals. Like the game we played as children, I was tagged "it."

Thankful I was only "temporary," I requested the afternoon off. My manager called after me, "I understand. I have children of my own."

I smiled as I drove to Strawberry Hill. "Yes, I have children; but this is no child, son, this is my adult, about-to-be divorced daughter, about your age." I paraphrased the old saying "a mother is a mother all her life" and put my positive thoughts into high gear.

Three days at Strawberry Hill blurred into one long daze. A feverish daughter, two boisterous grandsons, piles of laundry, cooking, and cleaning, cleaning, cleaning.

It all came back to me. The days of peanut butter and jelly sandwiches, small boys scrambling on bunk beds, now cowboys, now spacemen, now ferocious animals. Refrigerator doors opening and closing countless times a day, kitchen floors bearing the brunt of spilled milk, children constantly knocking at the front door, sounds of quarrels and slamming doors. Yes, it all came back in a flash.

Added to all this confusion was the sound of powerful bulldozers, scarcely a hundred feet to the rear of Nancy's home, plowing and tearing at virgin ground, splitting the air, felling trees from their age-old roots. Acres of land were being cleared for new residences. From dawn's early light to the setting of the sun, ear-splitting sounds disturbed what quiet there might have been. Air conditioning, something that had become a standard luxury to me, would have drowned out most of this noise; but Nancy's house was not equipped. Instead, open doors and windows beckoned the heat and the roaring noise into the house.

The noise and the dust from the construction were annoying, but tolerable. The other result of the construction, however, was not tolerable; it was harrowing. Frightened field mice, scampering through tall grass, racing for food and shelter, found their way into the homes at Strawberry Hill. These tiny creatures gnawed at boards, scratched at cupboards, and ran at high speed across kitchen floors and once (ugh) over my bare foot. My sense of humor took a speedy leave of absence; Nancy's quickly filled the void.

"Oh, come on, mom, they're only mice," she giggled. But I, who had bravely survived tornados in the Midwest and earthquakes in California, trembled at the sound of pattering feet.

As usual, whenever I found myself in a helpless situation, I called my husband.

"Lay traps," he instructed nonchalantly from our mice-free home thirty miles away. "Put a tiny piece of cheese on each one. You do have traps there, don't you? No? Well, go to the drugstore and . . ."

I swallowed. I couldn't complete the picture of me actually touching a trapped mouse, but I stubbornly refused to allow those tiny creatures to do me in. And I dared not allow my fear to affect my grandsons. So, on the defense, adrenaline flowing, I charged forward. My weapon was a large broom. To the cheers of Josh and Kevin, I chased the furry beast around the kitchen. But in a flash of fur my target disappeared, scurrying under the floorboard. Frustrated, I fell onto a chair, broom in hand, and couldn't decide whether to laugh or cry. We all decided to laugh.

Sleep eluded me that night. As moonlight poured through the window, my ears strained, waiting for the rolling thunder (or so it seemed) of gnawing and scratching. Covers pulled snugly over my head, face buried in my pillow, sleep, accompanied by dreams of Mickey Mouse dancing in step with Fred Astaire up the wall and upside down on the ceiling, at last overtook me.

On Saturday Vern arrived. He walked about the house spreading a white powder and setting traps. Before a week was over, the mouse problem disintegrated. As usual, Vern knew what to do and did it, faithfully fulfilling the role my generation had created for him—a knight, charging forward to rescue helpless maidens like me.

I was beginning to realize I had passed this faulty image on to Nancy, making it more difficult for her to adjust to being independent. For now there was no one to race to assist her when piles of trash needed to be lugged to the curb, when the TV set went black, when appliances broke down. Chores knew nothing of missing knights.

Driving home, I was of two minds. I was thankful to be near Nancy and to be able to help her through an emergency, but I realized the arrangement would be permanent for at least three more years. My temporary job would not provide the kind of financial help she would need. I would have to climb out of my hammock and back into the full-time job market.

This, I sighed, was part of being tagged "it."

Chapter 11

Nine to Five

Easing myself back into the job market the previous year as a temporary secretary had acquainted me with the latest advancements in technology. My office memories of manual typewriters, dial telephones, and papers cranked on ancient copiers were replaced by word processors, push button telephones, and Xerox machines that whirled out copies by the hundreds in quick succession. In moving from company to company as a temporary employee, I had gained expertise on much of the sophisticated equipment of the 80s. I was ready to interview for a permanent position.

"Managers are so young," I said to Vern after a day of interviewing.

"You're just seeing them through different eyes, honey," my diplomatic husband responded.

"Oh." I dimmed my dressing-table light to a soft rosy glow and dropped the subject.

After several more days of interviews with young managers, I finally accepted a position in a computer programming firm. Surrounded by logical and rational thinkers skilled in problem-solving and mathematics, I soon realized I was out of my league. Math and I, never compatible, now did battle over page after page of financial reports. And one look at my pencil was proof that math had won. It had been sharpened down to a stub, and the eraser refused to obliterate one more figure. I decided I'd better come clean and admit that I barely passed grade school math.

"Some people simply do not like math," my mathematician boss said, turning pale. "You just weren't taught properly." He rose to the occasion, walked to the blackboard, and before my astonished eyes began a basic math lesson that continued through the morning. Fearing that my superficial knowledge of mathematics would be disclosed, I forced my stunned brain to function at a higher level. The world of data processing and the non-language jumble of computers apparently was not my cup of tea; yet I had given my word when interviewed to stay for at least one year, so I focused my thoughts toward that end.

Admittedly, I had times of resentment. Friends were planning trips to exotic places and returning with glamorous photos. This was the time of life when Vern and I should have been thinking of retirement, quiet evenings alone, investing in a summer home, or moving to a smaller condo with tennis courts and swimming pools. I felt cheated.

Were we making right decisions? Should we simply have turned our back on Nancy's problems? We weighed the issues, reflected, and prayed, but in the end we came to the same conclusion—what we were doing was right for us, even though the same course of action might not be right for others.

Many divorced women had no options. Nancy's friend Patty was struggling to raise five children. Reluctantly she was making plans to move out of state to be closer to her parents. My divorced friend Marilyn said many times how disappointed she was that she couldn't pursue her education because she had so little physical and financial help. "It's nearly impossible to be a full-time student and mother unless someone is backing you," she had said. Her words reinforced my decision to work. Yet each morning as I left for the office, I glanced back at the unopened *Los Angeles Times,* remembering all the quiet, leisurely times I'd spent relaxing over a second cup of coffee.

I made up essays in my mind and called them *Divorce Is a Family Affair.* But the time to write them down, like time to stroll unhurried through shopping malls and to lunch with friends while chatting away the afternoon, was a luxury that was no longer mine.

Divorce clearly was not a drama with two leading characters. It required a supporting cast, and we, Nancy's family, had unwittingly been thrust into those roles.

Although I showed a smiling face to the world, anger simmered inwardly. Finally, my anger turned to depression and my depression to fatigue. In particular, I remember one Friday night after a long and difficult day at the office. I began to cry and I cried until my tears became uncontrollable sobs. My down elevator was speeding to the very lowest floor.

Neither Vern nor Dave, who stopped by at that inappropriate moment, could say anything that would stop my weeping. In desperation, Dave disappeared up the stairs.

"Mom," he said just a few minutes later, "there's someone on the phone for you."

Dave had called Dr. Willard. Although I would not have phoned him, once more God had sent him my way. As I had seen in the past and would see many times in the future, God, our loving Father, uses His willing children to comfort their brothers and sisters in times of distress. Dr. Willard's deeply sensitive manner brought an outpouring of my fears, my weariness, my depression.

"You're going to have to take a different view of God," he said gently, "and see your children in His hands."

I sniffled my answer.

"You've been carrying Nancy's load and your family's load, and now God has let you paint yourself into a corner and let you see how helpless you are. That's good. He wants you to *see* your inability to carry any burden, even your own."

The conversation went on, but what I replayed in my mind that night was the truth that I had painted myself into a corner. By nursing hurting hearts, trying to manage a full-time job and run my home with efficiency, I had brought on a classic case of burn out. My body's yellow warning light was flashing, cautioning me that it was time to slow down and put on the brakes.

I, who had written a book dealing with releasing one's children to God, had been clutching Nancy and her sons with titanic force. I knew I must let go. I must create a new visual picture, of my children in God's hands, being cared for by Him as Father, Husband, and Shepherd. If I did not let go, God would lovingly take them from my hand. I had experienced that once before and I did not wish to relive it.

Dear Lord, my foolish strivings are meaningless, like running in place. You who hold the wind in Your fists and wrap the ocean in Your cloak, are You not able to carry these burdens? Spread a table in my wilderness, Lord. I need still waters and green pastures. And thank You for gently teaching me that it is not circumstances that need changing, but me. Amen.

I realized my own life had been off balance since the day of Nancy's phone call. Like a juggler, I was trying to keep ten balls in the air at once, an impossibility if I was to remain physically and mentally well. Some of those balls would have to be put aside. I began to entertain the idea of throwing out the most frustrating one of all—my job. Yes, I decided, right after the first of the year, I would leave the professional world and perhaps begin writing again.

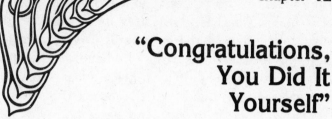

Chapter 12

"Congratulations, You Did It Yourself"

The time had come for Nancy to initiate divorce proceedings. After consulting with attorneys, she decided to do it herself. Divorce, so common, so uncomplicated according to California law, demanded only that both partners agree on property settlement and child support. Six months after signing the necessary papers, the marriage would be dissolved.

In looking back, I suppose I was hoping that in those six months Doug would realize his mistake, come home, and cancel the proceedings. No such thing happened, and by fall the papers were ready to be filed. In September, Nancy and her friend Patty made the short trip to the courthouse and picked up the papers.

As I noted the date on my calendar, tears filled my eyes. Our second daughter, Kathi, had been killed in an automobile accident on the same date many years before. Now another death had taken place, the death of a marriage. Perhaps not a death—that had already occurred; today the marriage was buried. But this time there was no graveside to leave behind. As bitterly final as death is, at least it *is* final. Unlike death, divorce, though final legally, still leaves room for hope. As long as there are children and the divorced couple continues to see each other, there is a possibility that the marriage may be resurrected.

"How easy it is to sign your name and wipe out ten years of your life," Nancy sighed. "This afternoon I walked around the neighborhood, looked at the homes with their families together, and wanted to cry, 'Why me? Look at me, I'm a divorced woman.'" She paused. "How I hate that word."

I could think of nothing to say.

"At the courthouse the woman handed me a decree. Do you know what the letter inside said? 'Congratulations, you did it yourself.' What a thing to be congratulated for. They call it the dissolution of a marriage; but no matter what words are used, it is terrible."

Unable to think of any appropriate words of wisdom, I expressed my love for her, which, I am sure, was all she wished to hear at that moment.

In the past two years, her faith had grown, outdistancing my own. Nancy was firmly trusting God. Physical problems had plagued her for a time, but now she was juggling a full load of college classes and handling the children as well.

Money continued to be her greatest need. Even though Doug was providing child support, her allotment would not stretch to meet the rising cost of living.

Although she was dating frequently, she found that rejoining the single world was like sailing a ship into strange waters. "It's like being a teenager again, only now I have to worry about a babysitter, rush home, and plunge into my mother role. I'm not sure it's worth the effort."

Starting over was definitely an uphill struggle. But since it was almost Christmas again, we put off thoughts of starting over until after the New Year.

After weeks of the usual flurry of shopping and baking, our family gathered for our traditional Christmas Eve buffet and to present gifts to one another. It was hard to believe that Josh was nearly nine this year and Kevin was six. Nancy and I sat down together before the still brightly lit fire after the house was quiet.

"Isn't it strange," she said softly, "how far God has brought me? I was an ordinary housewife and mother, safe and content in my very small world. Now, here I am, a science major, meeting interesting people and learning that I can become independent. It won't be long before I find my wings and feel that it's OK to be *me*, a single woman."

I nodded, fully understanding that single women often did not feel OK. Part of the blame could be placed on a society that was created for couples. It was not easy as a single; there were many places a lone woman did not go simply because she was alone.

Yes, I too longed for the day when she would win her wings.

And I wouldn't mind a new pair for myself as well.

Chapter 13

Where Am I and How Did I Get Here?

I had been thinking for some time that I would write a book on the empty nest syndrome, sharing experiences of parents who had had large families and who were suddenly "two" again. After over thirty years of raising five children and coping with each problem a mother faces every day, I felt duly qualified.

I was ready to write about the lessons we had learned and the bittersweet, happy-sadness of the empty nest.

But each time I wrote a chapter or two, one of our sons came back to the nest; it was a cold and costly world out there, and home looked better and better. So I had put my manuscript away.

Now, however, seemed the ideal time to begin again. Rich had purchased his own townhouse. Dave was living with Nancy, and Dan had moved closer to UCLA. I had quit my job at the beginning of the year, promising myself I would take a few months off to do some things that had been too long neglected. Perhaps I would even write a bit on *The Empty Nest*.

Top priority, though, was to refurbish our home now that there were just two of us. Children's fingerprints and dirty socks were a thing of the past. I finally could choose delicate, light fabrics without worrying about a child's mishap. So I chose lacy white curtains to grace our picture window and a bright floral sofa and two gold velvet chairs to complete the living room. Since we seldom used the room except for special occasions, it seemed reasonable to assume that gold and white would be practical. Next we redecorated our upstairs bedrooms, which for years had resembled a boys' dormitory. Footballs, baseballs, bats and mitts, tall hockey sticks, and skis were all gone forever. I was as pleased as a kitten with a saucer of fresh cream. Into our new guest room went white lace and eyelet bedspreads and matching curtains. After the wallpaper in a beige and brown dogwood pattern was added, my new room could have competed with any page straight out of *Better Homes and Gardens*. In my imagination, guests would love this room, and it would stay beautiful forever. No one would touch or mar the walls or spreads.

And at last I created a study of my very own—a longed-for place to write—a dream come true. Into the study went an executive desk and my faithful typewriter. I fancied spending long hours there with soft music playing in the background, echoing through the empty rooms. I would finish writing *The Empty Nest*.

Vern and I relished our aloneness, eating when we pleased or not eating at all. We were just two again, and we smiled luxuriantly in our new-found freedom.

How our dream-like life faded away into the mist, I'm not at all sure.

As close as I can remember, the chain of events went like this.

Nancy called one evening, her voice filled with despair. She had received a note from Josh's teacher saying his grades were failing and his attitude was beginning to manifest some inner hurts.

"I sat on the edge of the bed after I read the note," Nancy said, "and told the Lord that now that He was their Father He would have to solve this problem. The new semester starts next week and my lab classes will be long and hard. I don't really know what I'll do with the boys . . ."

We discussed various possibilities, but each option met a dead end. Solution after solution led to obstacles we couldn't climb. What, I wondered, do single parents do when they're attempting to finish their educations and care for small children at the same time?

"Wouldn't it be wonderful," I mused half to myself, "if the boys could attend the Christian academy?"

The West Valley Christian Academy was one block from our home, and each time I drove by I thought of Josh and Kevin. Academically and spiritually the school was rated tops. But there was a waiting list—probably another unrealistic solution.

"How could they?" Nancy asked. "I'd have to drive them in each day, drive back for my classes, pick them up at night. And isn't there a waiting list there?"

We turned the subject to other matters. But God, who had promised to be a Father to Nancy's sons, was gently leading and answering her plea for help. As we have come to discover, He works quietly and sometimes quickly. Often, while we are puzzling over a situation, He has already solved it. And isn't that what Isaiah 65:24 implies? "Before they call, I will answer; . . ."

That evening I was talking on the telephone to my friend Pat, a teacher at the academy. I casually mentioned my conversation with Nancy about Josh and Kevin attending the academy. I hastened to add, however, that I knew there was a waiting list and that it was an impossibility.

After a long silence, Pat said thoughtfully, "One of my kindergartners moved away, just today. There might be an opening for Kevin. Let me talk to the principal tomorrow."

I tossed and turned throughout the night. Something kept nagging at the back of my mind. When I finally did sleep, I dreamed of long roads that took me nowhere and winding dirt paths that led to mountainous areas where long lines of cars waited for a vast stone gate to open.

Pat called the following evening. She had spoken to the principal, who, though she had never met Nancy, felt a definite heart tug to talk with her. Could Nancy see her the next day?

We were stunned. "I suppose I should talk to her," Nancy said, "although I don't see how it would be possible . . ." Her voice trailed away, and into my mind came the clear picture I had tried in vain to erase. "God," I whispered, "You must be mistaken. I couldn't have them come live with us, not now, not with my freshly decorated rooms and our new furniture. Lord, I've had my share of children. You wouldn't ask this of me, would you?"

But He *was* asking, and I could find no peace until I listened obediently. I sighed. "There's really only one solution, Nancy," I finally said. "You and the boys could move in with us until you're out of college. Then they can attend the academy and . . ."

"I couldn't, mom. You and dad deserve to be alone. Do you know what it's like with two small boys?"

Me? I had raised five children; at one time, three of the boys had been under four years of age. Was she asking if *I* knew what it was like? Who knew better? But I also knew there was no other option. Although it must have been just as difficult for Nancy as it was for me, she, too, knew there was no other choice if she was to receive her degree and if the boys were to have proper supervision.

The new wings I had prayed for on Christmas Eve suddenly took flight—but without me. Instead, they took off with my plans for a leisurely, just-the-two-of-us, write-when-you-want-to lifestyle and left me alone with a very old, very worn out pair that I knew could never get me off the ground.

And yet, I had an unspeakable sense of well-being, simply because I was doing what God was asking of me. When I talked to Vern, his face reflected my feelings. Yet we both agreed it seemed the only viable solution. We would become extended parents for our grandsons, who were so in need at this most impressionable time in their lives.

And so it was decided. The principal of the academy met with Nancy and the boys and felt strongly that they should begin immediately. Monday? Only three days away!

We had a February rainstorm that weekend that defied anyone to attempt outdoor feats, yet Vern and Dave packed and moved Nancy's belongings into our home. Our garage became a storehouse. My lovely, redecorated guest room became Nancy's room.

"The Lord knew," she grinned, "even when you were decorating this room, that beige and brown are my favorite colors and that I would love the peaceful feeling of the lovely climbing dogwood.

Josh and Kevin shared a room, Dave was back home, and once more our house was full.

"Mom," Dave said at one point when I must have looked discouraged, "there's no greater calling than what you and dad are doing for Nancy and the boys. Nothing you ever do will exceed what these years will mean to them."

My mind agreed, but my emotions were still off balance.

The day Vern and Dave moved Nancy's belongings to our home, I switched on the television and heard a pastor say, "When your children are grown and you feel as though you've blown it with them, the very best you can do is pray; the impressionable years are gone, but . . ." and his eyes twinkled, "sometimes God gives us a second chance with our grandchildren."

I sighed. "Well, Lord, I guess I didn't shape up with five children, so I take it I need a couple more to undo some mistakes.

Chapter two began. Once more it was baseball mitts, soccer balls, beaten-down grass in the front yard where the neighborhood children gathered, batches and batches of laundry, and children's toys on the stairway. I had entered a time machine and gone back to another era in my life.

One night my friend Pat and I were chatting in my refurbished living room. "It's beautiful," she said, looking around the room. As I was thanking her, I stopped in mid-sentence. We both saw it at the same time. There on my large and lovely plant on the fireplace hearth hung a dirty sock.

"You can always call one chapter in your book 'What's that Dirty Sock Doing on My Plant?'" she suggested. "Kind of like 'Please Don't Eat the Daisies.'" We giggled as I gingerly picked up the sock and deposited it in the never-ending laundry pile—and I remembered a day not so long ago when I thought my days of children's dirty socks were a thing of the past.

I remembered assuring Nancy that of course I knew what it was like having small children around. Now, however, I was realizing that knowing and remembering are very different. My, how much I had forgotten. But every day new things happened that made me feel like I was living a continual instant replay, forcing me to remember what I had neatly stored away in my memory.

Josh's and Kevin's first day of school was one example. Since Nancy had early classes that day, it was left up to me to see that the boys were properly enrolled. Together we sloshed through the streets in the pouring rain. When we walked through the doors of the school and I took my first breath, I laughed out loud. The distinctive smell of classrooms sent my mind back to the day when I had enrolled our oldest son in kindergarten. With two preschoolers in tow, I had completed all the necessary forms and had gotten our son settled. The relief of having one son in school and only two at home was welcome, but I anxiously awaited the day they all would be in school. Now here I was, years later, enrolling two more. I sloshed back home, changed into dry clothes, and silently gazed through the window at the large raindrops falling outside. "Lord," I sighed, "where am I and how did I get here?"

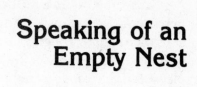

Chapter 14

Speaking of an Empty Nest

Late one Saturday afternoon, Vern and I were home alone watching Wide World of Sports on television—at least that's what Vern was doing. I was meditating on our step-saver kitchen. The rest of the house had been refurbished, but what we desperately needed now was a larger kitchen to accommodate our extended family.

I rose from my easy chair and walked around the small space, plotting how it could be accomplished. We had talked around the subject several times during our eighteen years in this home, but dollar signs had kept us from reaching a conclusion. Now the thought of six of us in a kitchen barely large enough for two made me ransack the corners of my mind for a creative alternative.

There must be a way!

"What if . . ." I said to Vern, who was intently watching the last few seconds of a basketball game. "What if you moved this bar out about four feet and? . . ."

He turned to look. Then turned back to the television set.

If anything, as my husband is well aware, I am persistent. I graciously waited until the final buzzer and then began tugging at the counter bar. Vern grimaced, sighed, and reluctantly came to look. We viewed that wooden bar from every angle, then began tugging to loosen it from its hinges. In minutes the bar was free.

We rotated slowly around the kitchen, mentally moving this appliance here and that one there. Yes, the cupboards needed restaining. To my amazement, Vern began unscrewing cupboard doors, lifting them from their hinges, and carrying them to the garage. Had he taken leave of his senses or was he as obsessed as I? Before evening fell we had the cupboard doors off and were deciding what color to stain them.

"What if . . ." I began again, "What if we order new cupboards and—you know—order new ones, a new kitchen? . . ." I stammered.

He looked at me and back to the line of doors and nodded.

We were scheduled to leave for our vacation in Michigan the following week. The next day was Easter Sunday and our family was expected for dinner. Vern, in his uncharacteristic obsession, had loosened several cupboards from their flooring, and they wobbled crazily.

The week before our vacation we discussed kitchen designs with experts, consulted with plumbers, and purchased a garden window, which, I explained hastily, would bring more sunlight into our kitchen and add dimension.

We left for Michigan with everything ordered so that on returning we could delve into the task of installing new cupboards.

If ever there is a contest to see how quickly a kitchen can be remodeled, we definitely feel we have a chance to win. On returning to California, everything was waiting for us, so Vern began work immediately by ripping out the window, fully expecting to install the garden window with the ease the manufacturer had promised. Not so! There, refusing to budge, was a solid pipe. Vern groaned. An emergency call to the plumber was of no help. He simply advised us to forget it and left.

My dream of a garden window was quickly going out the window when our son Dave appeared, looked over the situation, and announced, "Dad, I believe we can do it." They did! He stayed with Vern, ripping out cupboards and installing new ones as though they were on a television commercial (minus the smiles of course).

I stayed discreetly out of the way, emerging only to offer food from fast food restaurants or whatever I could create from the appliances on the dining room table.

As is often the case in construction projects, we found that one thing after another called for more changes—the appliances needed to be refinished to match the new almond ceramic tile, and, of all things, the air conditioning unit needed to be removed to install the garden window. So there we were, in the middle of a blistering hot California heat wave, trying primitive ways to stay cool while the smog and heat poured into the house along with the plumbers, electricians, and workmen who wandered in and out.

To escape the noise and dust and sheer craziness, I often fled to my room and my typewriter to continue writing on a new book on how divorce affects the family. (Once again I had put aside *The Empty Nest.*)

One day when the uproar was particularly wild, Nancy and I were sitting on the stairway for a moment's rest, attempting to converse above the noise of the grinding and pounding in the kitchen, when the doorbell rang. Assuming it was another workman, I nonchalantly called, "Come in."

A burly man entered, walking straight toward us.

"Do you like pizza?" he asked, beginning what was obviously a rehearsed speech.

"What? . . ."

"Yes, I'm selling two-for-one coupons for Delight Pizza. We deliver. We have the best pizza in town. For only seven dollars you can buy the whole book."

Nancy and I looked at each other and burst into laughter. I'm sure our sudden outburst coupled with the confusion all around us made him think he had walked into a very unstable household. To convince him that we really were quite normal and since we had been wondering what we would feed everyone for supper, we bought his coupons. That night we sat down to a feast of Delight Pizza, the worst pizza in town!

The moment the Armstrong linoleum was laid, we cheered the completion of our kitchen. Another page from *Better Homes and Gardens*. During that seven-day project I wondered why I had decided to leave my quiet nine-to-five job. And why had I believed being a housewife was "laid back"? But, of course, that was when I had assumed it was just going to be the two of us.

I would go back to work, however. Vern was beginning to mourn the demise of our savings account.

All in favor?

Aye!

And so, once more I joined the nine-to-five mainstream, this time as an administrative assistant to the vice-president of a major savings and loan corporation. I soon discovered, however, that I liked banking even less than I liked computer-programming. But God kept whispering, "Now is not forever." I tried to convince myself those words had meaning. At least, I said to myself, I can be grateful that life has settled into a semblance of order—Josh and Kevin were progressing wonderfully in the academy, and Nancy was studying hard and earning high grades.

Our extended family was finally working!

Chapter 15

Making a List and Checking It Twice

I would love to be able to say that my faith never wavered and that I moved forward, never back, in a rosy bloom of growth. But the hard truth is that my faith did fluctuate and my humanness became very evident. No, I did not always soar like an eagle above the circumstances. The image I had so carefully created of my children being held securely in God's hands was nearly always out of focus. Something was wrong!

I couldn't sleep at night. No matter how weary my body, my mind raced to my worry list, checking each item to make sure I had been sufficiently anxious throughout the day. Of course, I didn't call it a worry list. After all, it was my motherly duty to fret so that our family could hold together. There was so *much* to vex over. Nancy's health, for instance. What if something should happen to her? And what about medical insurance for her family? This was another very practical problem single women face. What if the boys were to become seriously ill and need hospitalization? I gave this priority on my worry list.

Would Nancy remarry? She was dating more frequently. How would the boys adjust to another man? Would he be good enough for her? What if she should face another marriage failure?

And her home. Could she afford to keep it? Even though she had never advertised for renters, a lovely and reliable couple had called to ask if they could have first choice. Still, I felt I should keep her home on my list and worry about it from time to time.

My health! What was wrong with me? I was tired so much of the time. And, of course, there was the health of my husband. Although he was as healthy as any man could be, one never knew. It was a good item to keep on the list—just in case.

This was not a prayer list, mind you. All of these worries should have been released to God. Instead, I had created a mental list and was checking it twice, once during the day and again at night as I lay sleeplessly tossing and turning.

Negative thought after negative thought invaded my mind. And I still didn't know what I was doing to myself or to those about me. Feeding on all my "what ifs" and "supposes," I kept my tiny, grain-of-mustard-seed faith firmly held in my tightly clenched hand, refusing to plant it in God's freshly plowed field.

And my body accommodated my thoughts by becoming ill. A severe bout with bronchitis kept me in bed for a week, and chronic laryngitis followed, making it difficult to use my voice. I worried about what illness could have caused my voice to soften and sometimes disappear. All medical opinions concurred. Tension.

Oh! Faith, where had I left you? And when? I remembered the words of Jesus, "Take no thought for the morrow."

But, my goodness, if I didn't take thought for tomorrow who would? Certainly no one else in this house was carrying such a load as I?

My inner spirit rebelled at my situation, though outwardly I refused to confess I wasn't where I wished to be in my life. My carefully laid plans had gone awry. I couldn't even remember what they were. Night after night, after returning home from work, I choked back resentment that our house was full, our dining room table fully extended. It was unfair. I had paid my dues, hadn't I?

The least Nancy could do would be to help me fret. She refused. She kept a little motto on her desk, "God is faithful, who will do it."

Even Vern wouldn't cooperate and worry along with me. It was all my burden to bear.

God finally reached me through a friend in a strange way. She was praying one day when my name came distinctly into her mind along with a message she felt God would have her give me. She called and said, "I don't understand what this means, but I must say it to you. 'Unless the heart is clean and right, the manifestation will not be clean and right.'"

I understood clearly, even though she did not. The Spirit of God had spoken directly to me. Tears flooded my face. How gentle God was to remind me that my heart needed cleansing. He had stopped me in my tracks, showing me my worry list as clearly as though it were on a screen. And just as a computer will code-cancel a document, through prayer I released my worry list, asking God to cancel each item.

I wish I could say the screen cleared overnight, but it didn't. I hung on to a few items, those I felt were worthy of my worry. And I still cannot honestly confess that all worry has vanished in a cloud of prayer. I can only say that when my focus is on Christ and my heart is in His Word, He erases anxiety and replaces it with peace.

I often read and re-read Philippians 4:6–8 from the *Living Bible:*

> Don't worry about anything; instead, pray about everything; tell God your needs and don't forget to thank Him for His answers. If you do this you will experience God's peace, which is far more wonderful than the human mind can understand. His peace will keep your thoughts and your hearts quiet and at rest as you trust in Christ Jesus. . . . Fix your thoughts on what is true and good and right. Think about things that are pure and lovely, and dwell on the fine, good things in others. Think about all you can praise God for and be glad about.

God's message to me. Replace my negative thoughts with the positive teaching of His Word. Think about what I could praise Him for. The list was endless—a loving, faithful husband; healthy children and grandchildren; a warm home; an abundance of all that we needed; children who had made decisions to follow the Lord; and other blessings too numerous to mention.

As I began to lean on the Lord, casting down my imaginations and fears, tension relaxed my ailing throat. Headaches disappeared.

"Come," Jesus said, "Come to me and I will give you rest." And all along, rest was what I had been searching for.

Chapter 16

Mothers and Others

Our problem was not unique. Everywhere I turned, it seemed, parents, like us, who had never dreamed it was possible, were stunned as their children's marriages broke up. Some took full responsibility for their grandchildren while the husband and wife went to "find themselves." Others brought their children and families into their homes. Some were blocked by bitter spouses from communicating with their beloved grandchildren.

Although the heartache is the same, God deals with each of us in diverse ways. What works for me may not work for others. He has an infinite imagination and knows our inner needs and how to work in our lives for our highest good.

Some beg, plead, and bargain with God to heal the broken marriages of their children; but still the break is final. What then? Some become bitterly resigned. Others quietly accept that their road has taken an unexpected turn. They realize, however, that God was not the author of this tragedy and did not will it, but that He is waiting to pick them up, dust them off, and assist them in starting over again.

How easy it is to argue over circumstances. How often I did just that. *"Why,* Lord, why did you let this happen?" But then I would remember a little verse tucked away in Romans that I have locked into my memory. "Oh, the depth of the riches of the wisdom and knowledge of God! How unsearchable his judgments, and *his paths beyond tracing out!"* (Rom. 11:33).

If I searched a million places to find out "why" it would be fruitless. Perhaps in eternity God will reveal the answer. But by then my faith will rest in His perfect ways after all.

Those who allow themselves to start over find that life can joyously continue. Their hearts have been made tender toward others in pain. They have learned from their mistakes.

Others, however, remain bitter.

I have seen sparks of hatred in the eyes of the rejected party toward an unfaithful spouse, a full-blown malice that ignites and destroys everything in sight.

I fully understand how this is possible, but it should not be so in the lives of God's children—those of us who have been freely forgiven and who have been commanded to forgive in the same manner. God's Word accurately states, "Watch out that no bitterness takes root among you, for as it springs up it causes deep trouble, hurting many in their spiritual lives" (Heb. 12:15 LB).

I know the parents of one divorced couple who

bitterly refused to forgive their ex-son-in-law for leaving their daughter. To this day, many years later, his name is not to be mentioned in their presence. Further, their anger extended to his parents. Accusations sparked their conversation. "If you had only been a different parent, your son would not have deserted our daughter."

Parents blame parents, forgetting that Cain and Abel were raised in the same home. Divisons occur, splitting families, even after both parties remarry.

And when children are involved, the problem becomes even more complex—the estrangement is carried one step further. Parents are not only separated from a son- or daughter-in-law, but from their beloved grandchildren as well if the custody parent moves out of town or refuses to allow the children to visit the parents of his or her ex-spouse. Suddenly, even though the grandparents may have been seeing their grandchildren as often as once a week, that close, loving relationship is severed. And holidays, which had once been so precious, become empty.

How tragic when children of divorce not only lose a parent, one of the two most important people in their lives, but their grandparents as well. But it is even more tragic when that relationship is broken unnecessarily. Perhaps the custody parent is simply waiting for some sign of interest from the grandparents, but never receives one because the grandparents have withdrawn into a cocoon of pain and suffering, fearing that in spite of their efforts they may never see their grandchildren again.

Other grandparents, however, although realizing

that possibility exists, continue to write letters, send birthday cards and gifts, and assure their grandchildren they are loved and remembered, thus keeping the lines of communication open for a future relationship.

The cycle of broken relationships is the heartbreaking tragedy of divorce. Although much has been written pleading with parents and grandparents not to allow children to become pawns, pride and selfishness often come before the needs of the children, thus perpetuating the cycle—and children are the losers once more.

One mother, a friend of mine, told me about another side of this tragic story—the frustration of parents who realize their child is about to make a dangerous mistake but who are helpless to prevent it. Her twenty-five-year-old son had fallen in love with and was planning to marry a thirty-four-year-old woman with three children. Though my friend liked the woman, she could foresee problems ahead.

"Just think," she said in sharing her concern about her son's relationship, "she was married twelve years, half his lifetime, before they met. We tried so hard to raise our children with proper principles and values, yet our daughter married a divorced man and is in an unhappy situation, and now our son . . ."

As I spoke with my friend my thoughts rebuked me—I was offering profound advice that I had not heeded. As my daughter began dating I myself began questioning her choice of companions. Was he stable? Kind? Did he love children? Would he be faithful? What about his faith? How deep was his commitment to God? But here I was, assuring my friend that we cannot and should not try to plan our children's lives—that their mistakes are theirs alone. But did I really believe that? As I drove home I prayed that I would learn.

> *Lord, teach me that what I have just said is true. Help me remember how You parent me, allowing me to miss the path You have for me, permitting me to make mistakes, standing by and picking me up when I fall. You are the perfect parent, Lord, and yet Your magnificent, nevertheless love gives me freedom to choose even to wander.*
>
> *Teach me to parent, Lord, during my parenting days and teach me how to stop when my parenting days are over. Amen.*

In most cases it seems that we mothers have the most difficulty accepting our children's pain. Doubtless, this is because we have nurtured and cared for their needs from the time they were babies. Like mother birds, we have hovered over our nests, feathering them and warming and cuddling our fledglings. When the time comes for them to make their first flight, we are hesitant to let them go, knowing the dangers they will face. And when the flight ends in a tragic nose dive, we blame ourselves because it has always been our responsibility to protect them.

Yes, we mothers remember the wedding day, the beautifully spoken vows, and the tenderness between the lovers who have become one and who sincerely believe that theirs is a forever love.

But when what we believed to be shatterproof, forever love suddenly breaks into a thousand pieces, we mothers, as well as our children, must pick up what we can salvage of our lives and go on. For just as surely as divorce shatters the life of the divorced person, it also shatters the life of the parents of the divorced.

Once My Child,
Now My Friend

When two families merge into one house, it is not as simplistic as I may have made it seem. Nancy had been mistress of her own home, a full-time mother and full-time wife, when she was thrust back in time. Suddenly she was a daughter again living in her parents' home.

It was a very difficult time of readjustment. We, who had been such good friends while living apart, grew hostile toward one another and our hurt festered into anger.

I finally realized that those unhappy times inevitably came when I unwittingly took back my role as her mother and did not allow her space as an adult woman.

I heard the statement, "Once my child, now my friend." I could not have it both ways. Biologically, Nancy was still my daughter; but emotionally, she had outgrown the need to be mothered. But mothering came to me as naturally as breathing. I often heard myself giving the identical instructions I

107

had given her when she was a teenager. Sparks flew, and suddenly we were not friends at all.

"Stop mothering me," she flared. "I'm a grown woman. I can't be a mother and a daughter at the same time."

I knew I must stop mothering and become a friend, ready with a listening heart when she felt like talking, silent when she wanted to keep her own counsel. Easy? No, but essential if we were to walk in harmony and to allow love to rule in our home.

One day at work I was venting my frustrations to a Christian co-worker who listened and then quoted these beautiful words from the Epistle of James.

> When all kinds of trials and temptations crowd into your lives, . . . don't resent them as intruders, but welcome them as friends! Realize that they come to test your faith and to produce in you the quality of endurance. But let the process go on until that endurance is fully developed, and you will find you have become a man of mature character with the right sort of independence (James 1:2–4 PHILLIPS).

When he left my office the words churned around in my mind, rushing back again and again, and finally settled into my heart. Trials were often sent by God as friends to produce endurance and to fully develop our character. I had been actively pushing them away as intruders, unaware that God meant them to bring me to maturity, to help me grow—no matter how costly or how much it hurt.

I got the message. My thirty-plus years of

mothering must come to an end. It was time to become friends with my children.

At times I still hear my mother-voice speaking words of well-meant wisdom and counsel to my children. But even in the midst of my much speaking, I see a glazed look come over their eyes and I realize what I'm doing.

And I can hear them thinking, "You're doing it again, mom."

I long to grow so that one day I can say, "You were once my child; now you are my friend," and so that I can listen to them as I would to a friend, offering not counsel, but a loving heart.

I admit, though, that I'm not there yet. I still have roads to travel, lessons to learn, tests to pass, and barriers to hurdle. But, "Since the Lord is directing our steps, why try to understand everything that happens along the way?" (Prov. 20:24 LB).

No, I don't understand. But now I know it's OK not to understand.

Parents our age have been outspoken. "I don't know how you stand having young children around the house again. We couldn't do it."

Silently I reply, "No, don't do it, not unless a very deep assurance settles in your heart that the Lord is directing your steps in that way. Then you must fully trust that He will give you every single grace you need for the second time around."

The time must come when not only we as parents must let go of our children, but our children must let go of us. It is damaging to allow our nest to become so comfortable that our children dare not fly away.

In the final analysis, I do believe that the very best God has for us as parents is the day our children stand alone and call us blessed—and call us their friends!

Chapter 18

Disconnecting

The day came over a year later when we instinctively knew it was time for Nancy to move into a place of her own. She was working part time, holding down a full load of studies, and we mutually felt it was possible and necessary, for all our well-being, for her to be on her own again. Nancy found a small, two-bedroom apartment close enough to Vern and me so we could still extend our support when needed.

The move was not easy for Josh and Kevin. An apartment complex is not the best of places for little boys to grow up. Once again they were uprooted from their neighborhood friends and from a home where they could run and play in the yard.

I prayed that Nancy's life would be full and rich and that the greatest of blessings and happiness would come to her and her children. But I could now see it was not *I* who could give that to her. And so I prayed intensely that God would bring renewal to her life. I even had to pray for wisdom to know how to pray.

Just about the time I added this request for Nancy to my prayer notebook, I was able to cross off one very special request for Dave, which God had answered beyond my expectations. Although it meant a kind of "disconnection" from another one of my children, I was extremely happy when Dave fell in love with a lovely young woman and married her in a beautiful spring ceremony. What a special and compassionate brother he had been to his sister. What a loving and thoughtful husband he would be. He, too, had matured tremendously through this experience, and his life and marriage would be enriched as a result.

During the wedding ceremony as my children stood together at the altar, I thought about married love, how it grows with the passing years when it is watered and tended. Love, fragile as a thread but strong as a rope, holds our lives together. No greater legacy can be given to our children than memories of a father and mother who love each other.

During the months that followed his marriage, of course, Dave had less time to spend with his sister and nephews, but somehow he *made* time for them. A trip to Disneyland, an overnight at Uncle Dave's house, a dinner, a romp with his dog. The investment he made in the lives of those two young boys is beyond measure.

Oh, yes, about my guest room.

As I was about to replace the lace and eyelet bedspreads I heard furniture moving upstairs. Dan, who had decided to move back home while finishing his last year at UCLA, was moving his stereo and comfortable chair into the spare room. He was furnishing a two-room apartment for himself. And my other spare room is reserved for those frequent nights when Josh and Kevin spend the night with us.

Which reminds me, "Now is not forever." There is a road ahead full of joyous and wondrous surprises.

We have been in the valley before and have emerged with greater strength. We had lost the precious gift of our second daughter, and God had turned that tragedy into great good. Nothing we as a family had gone through had been able to separate us from God's love, His peace, or His presence. And nothing ever would.

> I have become absolutely convinced that neither death nor life, neither messenger of Heaven nor monarch of earth, neither what happens today nor what may happen tomorrow, neither a power from on high nor a power from below, nor anything else in God's whole world has any power to separate us from the love of God in Christ Jesus our Lord! (Rom. 8:38–39 PHILLIPS).

Let me put it another way.

> I have learned with absolute certainty that nothing, not the death of a child nor the divorce of a child, not our humanness, not our lack of love, not our misunderstandings, not our dogmatism, not our frustrations, not our anger, not our lack of faith has any power to separate us from the absolute and incredible love that God has for His children through Christ Jesus our Lord.

Chapter 19

In Thinking It Over

Of course my vision is clearer now, but in looking back, I see many things I would have done differently. I should have called out for help when I was struggling to cross the rocky places. But I stubbornly refused, thinking I could make it alone, even though the mountains were much too high and steep and the valleys were much too low and dark for my unprepared feet.

At the beginning, when ominous signs appeared that Nancy's marriage was failing, I wish I had not denied what was happening. I wish I had faced the problem and suggested counseling for both of them and that they spend time praying together.

I'm grateful for the lesson God taught that we must not rush to judgment, but that we must wait until we are able, in faith, to make rational decisions.

Turning my anger inward and refusing to admit I was angry at the unexpected turn of events that changed our lives was a mistake. I should not have discounted my hostility, but examined it and dealt with it. I believe healing would have come sooner.

In looking back I see that withdrawing into a shell and wrapping Nancy's problems about me like a cocoon was also a mistake. I should have continued to enjoy a widely varied social life. Now I realize it was not so much that my friends withdrew from me, but that I slipped into a private, painful world of my own. In doing so, I isolated myself from the prayers and support of loving friends.

I wish I had not spent so much time debating the right or wrong of divorce. Obviously, it *is* wrong, but how much more profitable it would have been if I had admitted, "Yes, it is a sorry thing that has happened and terribly, terribly painful; but here it is . . ." How useless to go over and over the rights or wrongs and to have to prove one's position is "biblical." And I wish more was written from this approach. Theologians may never agree on this issue, but in the meantime we need people who will say, "OK, it has happened, now here is where you should go from here."

I learned that bargaining with God and playing my game of "if only You will do this, I will do that" does not work. God is not in the bargaining business. When Job cried out for answers, none were forthcoming. Indeed, God questioned *him*. I know now that God does not owe me an explanation.

I wish I had fed more on God's Word and less on my own and others' opinions and advice. Again and again during my spiritually dry periods, I needed to hear God's voice through His Word; yet often my ears were not listening.

I most assuredly learned that not all Christians hold the same views concerning divorce. But then, we do not all hold the same doctrinal views on many issues. That does not negate the fact that we are family and that we are commanded to love one another whether we agree or disagree.

Nancy once wrote in her journal, "I envision myself as a caterpillar that is suddenly changed into a butterfly. I can either fight the change and keep trying to crawl like a caterpillar or I can use my new wings and fly gracefully from flower to flower." I am so happy she decided to fly. Yes, she has certainly won her wings.

I, too, am finally flying with the new wings I ordered so long ago. I think they were probably there all along, but, like a new pair of shoes, sometimes they need to be worn awhile before they feel comfortable. And it was a long time before I was willing to "break them in." I kept trying to give them back to God with the message that they weren't the ones I had ordered—they didn't fit—they were too uncomfortable. But now they feel fine. And they have flown me to a vantage point from which I can see how Nancy's divorce changed my life for the better. I believe I was plunged back into the working world for a specific reason. Although I spent many restless days in positions I was not suited for, those experiences eventually opened the doors for me to work for a charitable organization in a field I love—writing and speaking. So the phrase God kept whispering to me, "Now is not forever," was not meaningless after all.

And, even more importantly, Nancy's divorce changed my life for the better spiritually. I know now that in the providence of God, He used Nancy's divorce to call a halt to my spiritual pride and prejudice and to teach me lessons I could not have learned any other way.

Just as Kathi's death taught me to reach out to bereaved parents, Nancy's divorce opened my eyes to see for the first time the terrible pain of children of divorce, single parents, parents of divorced children, estranged in-laws and grandparents, and the unbelievable fallout from a fragmented family.

Like a swimmer who had been safely clinging to a raft, I was pushed away from the security and forced to learn to swim in some very deep, murky waters. But now that I have learned to swim, I would not trade my freedom for any raft, and particularly not the one I had used for my security. For that raft was not my belief that divorce is wrong, it was my pride that all was well in our family because we had done everything right; and I should never have been clinging to it in the first place. Now I know that even when we do the very best we know to do at the time, our children may marry outside our pleasure, may never marry, may divorce, may rebel, may reject our values, may take and never give, may cruelly disappoint us until we feel as though God's blessing is forever removed. *It is not so!* God has pronounced a forever blessing on those of us who are "accepted in His beloved Son," and nothing can ever change it.

So, just as God accepted us in our less-than-desirable condition, I am learning, though more slowly than I would like, to accept others just where they are. If I am walking in the kingdom of God here and now, and I am, then I am to be salt and light to a hurting world. And a hurting world simply will not listen to an unaccepting person.

Sometimes when I look back at the stormy waters we crossed and think ahead to what might be, I wonder how we made it this far. The answer, of course, is that *we* have not. Underneath, all along, have been and are the everlasting arms.

Chapter 20

Letter to My Daughter

My dear daughter,

Now that you have moved out of our home, please never think that you have moved out of our care and concern. If anything, we think about you more now and of the difficult times that may be yours ahead. You and I have talked long about divorce, about your years with Doug, about your children and their future. We have wept together, especially in those first few months when the grief was so fresh. I was so much your mother *that I suffered each tiny pain with you.*

I'm sure you know that your divorce has been very difficult for dad and me and that we would give anything at all if it had not happened. But you can't know how I have prayed, asking God to bring your husband back to you and his sons. But because I do not know the ways of God, I cannot say why those prayers have not been answered. Perhaps they were answered, and I don't have eyes to see.

I know you hurt beyond what you can express. I know the times you excused yourself to go to your room very early, when you were weeping into your pillow. Though you didn't know it, I was weeping, too.

You told me you have freely forgiven Doug. I hope that is true, not only for his good, but for your own, too. For failing to forgive causes a small canker to become a cancer that will destroy healthy cells. You may have to forgive over and over again—forgive when you call to speak to him and she answers the telephone; forgive when he promises to take the boys for the weekend and then calls to cancel after you have made exciting plans; forgive when the money doesn't come in on time; forgive over and over until forgiveness becomes as natural as breathing. And you and I both know that this kind of forgiveness can only result from knowing how much God has forgiven us. The results of not forgiving show on people's faces, etching an ugliness into the soul and blocking the power of God's flow in their lives. So, I hope you will keep right on forgiving each time the wound is reopened.

You and I talked about not being able to understand something until one has gone through it. I agreed, and I still agree. I know I cannot understand your pain nor see from your perspective what this divorce has done to your life. But neither can you see from my perspective what it has done to me. We must each understand that. I have told this story as I have seen it. It might not be the way you saw it at all, but because it is a mother's story, I could only tell it from my own point of view. Forgive me, too, if I gave any pat answers or made things seem easy and rosy for you. How well I know that this has not been true. You have truly suffered. Understand that I cannot understand what you feel, but to the extent I can, I am sorry.

How I have loved your letters to the Lord. Thank you for sharing them with me. Keep writing to Him and keep waiting for His answers.

I lived with you long enough to know how incredibly hard

it is to be a full-time student, a mother, and a daughter. I see now that we were looking at the same situation from two different views, and that we were both right and both wrong.

I am sure that to be on your own is best for you—at least for now. As difficult as it is to make ends meet, you are standing, and I am proud of you! And because your self-esteem suffered so greatly through all this, you must feel greater pride in yourself now that you are doing what at one time seemed impossible. In future years, you will look back on these days and see more clearly the hand of God caring for you and your sons.

As your sons grow (and how quickly they are growing!), spend much time in prayer for their lives. Dad and I do. Pray that they will know God as their Father in a very special way and that they will honor and love and respect you for what you are sacrificing for them (for they cannot realize just how much you think of their well-being).

You have, dear Nancy, much to be thankful for—you have said it yourself over and over. As I write this letter, I think of how very good God has been in giving you brothers who have stood by through your most difficult days. I don't think you will ever know how to fully thank Dave for the year he lived with you and carried part of your burden. Wasn't he a beautiful picture of Christ, so strong and loving, to take cares from you and carry them so lightly? Now Dave is going forward with his new life as a married man. But even as the memory of that year dims, when you look back, remember his love.

You and I talked often of divorcees with children who do not walk closely with their Heavenly Father or who do not even acknowledge God at all. We have wondered what they do with their burdens. You and I have seen the results of those *spiritless lives. Thank God for His Holy Spirit, the Comforter, in our lives.*

You cannot know how hard it was for me to totally "let go." But can you see that I had to? So if at times I have seemed uncaring or busy in my own world, seemingly enjoying my life, understand that I, too, am a person and need to follow in the path God has for me. To be your friend eventually meant that I had to stop being your mother. Admittedly, it was not always easy to refrain from handing out advice when I thought you were making a mistake, but that, too, is part of "letting go."

You and I have also talked about all the "what ifs." It is time we let them go. We have sentimentalized about what if Kathi were here, how nice it would be if you had your sister now. Even though no one knows it, twelve years after our loss, I still weep for her. But that, too, is part of forgetting the past. We have to deal with where we are now.

I'm going to venture to talk a little about love, and please, these are only my thoughts. But more and more I sense, especially after my thirty-five years of marriage to your father, that love—this quiet love like your dad and I have for each other—far surpasses those first years of romance and passion. Who could sustain that kind of high anyway? But this kind of comfortable love is not a feeling, it is acts of love that we offer one another.

As someone so aptly phrased it, it is "nevertheless love"—the kind of love that keeps on loving in spite of dullness or lack of affection or selfishness or ill-temperedness.

I'd like to share with you what C. S. Lewis called "being in love."

What we call "being in love" is a glorious state, and, in several ways, good for us. It helps to make us generous and courageous, it opens our eyes not only to the beauty of the beloved but to all beauty, and it subordinates (especially at first) our merely animal sexuality; in that sense, love is the great conqueror of lust. No one in his senses would deny that being in love is far better than either common sensuality or cold self-centredness. But, as I said before, "the most dangerous thing you can do is to take any one impulse of our own nature and set it up as the thing you ought to follow at all costs." Being in love is a good thing, but it is not the best thing. There are many things below it, but there are also things above it. You cannot make it the basis of a whole life. It is a noble feeling, but it is still a feeling. Now no feeling can be relied on to last in its full intensity, or even to last at all. Knowledge can last, principles can last, habits can last; but feelings come and go. And in fact, whatever people say, the state called "being in love" usually does not last. If the old fairy-tale ending "They lived happily ever after" is taken to mean "They felt for the next fifty years exactly as they felt the day before they were married," then it says what probably never was nor ever could be true, and would be highly undesirable if it were. Who could bear to live in that excitement for even five years? What would become of your work, your appetite, your sleep, your friendships? But, of course, ceasing to be "in love" need not mean ceasing to love. Love in this second sense—love as distinct from "being in love" is not merely a feeling. It is a deep unity, maintained by the will and deliberately strengthened by habit; reinforced by (in Christian marriages) the grace which both parents ask, *and receive, from God. They can have this love for each other even at those moments when they do not like each other; as you love yourself even when you do not like yourself. They can retain this love even when each would easily, if they allowed themselves, be "in love" with someone else. "Being in love" first moved them to promise fidelity: this quieter love enables them to keep the promise. It is on this love that the engine of marriage is run: being in love was the explosion that started it.**

I pray this kind of love for you!

How and when God will answer or if He will answer in the way we expect, I cannot say.

But, in spite of the amputation of divorce, you have much joy ahead. Look for it. Don't let it slip away. Cling to joy no matter where you go.

And remember, time from God's perspective is much different than our moments and hours and days. He lives in the eternal now—yesterday, today, and tomorrow have all been lived, and He knows and remembers your address and is keeping a steady eye on you.

I am writing this letter exactly four years from the day you called me on that hot Sunday to tell me your marriage was over.

In these four years, I think you will agree that you and I have grown closer, and yet further apart; that we have understood and misunderstood; that we have learned much about God's grace, but that we still have much more to learn. As you have said, you have seen love in action from your family and friends and have marveled at the faithfulness of God in every single area of your life. Together, through all this, we have witnessed many miracles. But to me, the greatest miracle has been watching God take those shattered pieces of your life that you offered Him so long ago and make them into a beautiful vessel that reflects His love. Though excruciatingly painful, it always takes death to produce life!

Let us, you and me, pray that the pain you have gone through will produce much fruit in many, many lives. And perhaps God will even use the death of your marriage as a seed that will produce long, healthy marriages for many others.

Love always,

Your Mother